Acclaim for

Baby-Led Weaning

Winner of the National Parenting Publications Awards (NAPPA) Honors Award, 2011

"Hands off, mama! With baby-led weaning, your kid is in charge. It might be the best thing to happen in the high chair since the invention of the bib."

—***Parents***

"Cleanup aside, our adventure in self-feeding has been one of my favorite chapters in early parenthood. I've especially loved gathering around the dinner table together, and I'm proud of the curious, independent eater Emma (now a 1-year-old) has become."

—Julia Scirrotto, *The New York Times*

"Doing things [the BLW] way has three advantages: It puts off feeding until the baby is really ready . . . It puts the baby in charge of how much he eats . . . It also brings baby to the table and encourages family meals, and family meals are good for the health, development, and behavior of children as they grow."

—Claire McCarthy, MD, Harvard Health

"[Rapley and Murkett] encourage parents to forgo the usual baby puree and move straight to whole foods while continuing to breastfeed primarily after a baby is six months old. Their arguments are scientifically sound, especially when it comes to muscle development in the mouth, and they address the anticipated counterarguments. . . . If mine were little again, I would definitely try this. As long as mom is nursing, who says baby can't eat lamb chops?"

—*Library Journal*, starred review

"Instead of suffering through months of mashed vegetables all over the walls and playing annoying airplane games with a spoonful of green goop (does anyone really like those peas?) I was starting her off with scrambled eggs, avocado, melon and strawberries . . . [BLW] means introducing whole foods to the baby to foster her independence."

—Amy Klein, *Washington Post*

"Watching [baby Mirah] respond to the pleasures of ripe tomatoes, curried rice noodles, and all kinds of meats and vegetables has made mealtime a much more enjoyable experience for all three of us. We can tell she is learning through all of her senses . . . and since we are generally sharing the same meal, I am more likely to make us all something healthy."

—Aimee Pohl, Babble.com

"It sounds like common sense: After all, would you want to be strapped into a high chair and force-fed spoon after spoon of bland vegetables? It's surely much more exciting to be able to exercise a bit of control over your diet."

—*Guardian*

"[Baby-led weaning] is where you put chunks of food out for them and they just sort of smash it around and throw it . . . but they build a relationship with food, and they eventually get some stuff in. They've got the bottle and then they wean themselves off the bottle because they get more food."

—Lucy Liu, on *Jimmy Kimmel Live!*

"My husband and I are pretty darn happy [with BLW] because it means we can actually sit down to a hot meal together, rather than take turns spoon-feeding a child, while dinner gets cold . . . I believe this sense of exploration also helped my boys be open to new foods, tastes, and textures."

—Andree Lau, editor-in-chief, *HuffPost Canada*

"The potential benefits of BLW don't end with ditching purees. It's proposed that this self-feeding approach may improve parental feeding practices (to be less controlling), support an infant's ability to self-regulate her intake (making the child more responsive to hunger and fullness cues), increase overall family meal quality, reduce picky eating and promote faster fine motor skill development and feeding skill confidence."

—Leslie Schilling, *U.S. News & World Report*

"Much like baby-led nursing, baby-led weaning puts your baby in charge of what, when, and how much they eat, letting them explore different foods and, ultimately, become tiny, non-picky connoisseurs." **—Olivia Youngs, Romper**

"I've been telling mothers for years that when babies start grabbing food from the table, they are ready for solids. I had the pleasure of observing this with my own children. What I love about this book is the joy and zest the authors put into parenting, their commonsense approach, and their faith that babies will do the right things for themselves when the time is right. Baby-led weaning is easy, and it makes parenting fun!"

—Nikki Lee, RN, MS, IBCLC

"Gill Rapley's work is amazing and makes so much sense. I recommend this groundbreaking book to every new mother I know. Read it. It will forever change the way you think about feeding your baby."

—Kathleen Kendall-Tackett, PhD, IBCLC, clinical associate professor of pediatrics, Texas Tech University School of Medicine, and coauthor of *Breastfeeding Made Simple*

"For my baby-led-weaner and me, BLW took the chore out of solids, and put the joy back in—and gave me just the excuse I needed to put down the hand-held blender. . . . I knew all of this because I'd read *Baby-Led Weaning* by Gill Rapley and Tracey Murkett, the bible for BLW parents." **—Andrea Mara, *Irish Independent***

"No purees, no ice cube trays, no food processor, no potato masher . . . just you and your child, eating food that you enjoy . . . [my baby] *adored* feeding herself while her parents ate their own meals. I can't even begin to tell you how pleasant it is to eat in a restaurant with your baby-led weaning child chomping on a piece of bread and butter or a chunk of cucumber from your salad beside you."

—Aitch, founder of Babyledweaning.com

BABY-LED WEANING

Also by Gill Rapley and Tracey Murkett

The Baby-Led Weaning Cookbook—Volume 2: 99 More No-Stress Recipes for the Whole Family

Baby-Led Breastfeeding: Follow Your Baby's Instincts for Relaxed and Easy Nursing

The Baby-Led Weaning Cookbook: Delicious Recipes That Will Help Your Baby Learn to Eat Solid Foods—and That the Whole Family Will Enjoy

BABY-LED WEANING

THE ESSENTIAL GUIDE

How to Introduce Solid Foods and Help Your Baby to Grow Up a Happy and Confident Eater

---

COMPLETELY UPDATED AND EXPANDED
10TH ANNIVERSARY EDITION

Gill Rapley, PhD, AND Tracey Murkett

NEW YORK

Baby-Led Weaning: *The Essential Guide—How to Introduce Solid Foods and Help Your Baby to Grow Up a Happy and Confident Eater—Completely Updated and Expanded 10th Anniversary Edition*

Originally published in the UK as *Baby-Led Weaning* by Vermilion, an imprint of Ebury Publishing/ Random House Group, in 2008. First published in North America in revised form by The Experiment, LLC, in 2010 by arrangement with Vermilion. This second edition has been updated and revised.

The Experiment, LLC | 220 East 23rd Street, Suite 600, New York, NY 10010-4658
theexperimentpublishing.com

Library of Congress Cataloging-in-Publication Data

Names: Rapley, Gill, author. | Murkett, Tracey, author.
Title: Baby-led weaning : the essential guide how to introduce solid foods
and help your baby to grow up a happy and confident eater / Gill Rapley,
PhD, and Tracey Murkett.
Description: Updated and expanded Tenth Anniversary edition. | New York : The
Experiment, 2019. | Includes bibliographical references and index. |
Identifiers: LCCN 2019002976 (print) | LCCN 2019003911 (ebook) | ISBN
9781615195596 (ebook) | ISBN 9781615195589 (pbk.)
Subjects: LCSH: Infants--Weaning. | Infants--Nutrition. | Baby foods.
Classification: LCC RJ216 (ebook) | LCC RJ216 .R335 2019 (print) | DDC
649/.33--dc23
LC record available at https://lccn.loc.gov/2019002976

ISBN 978-1-61519-558-9
Ebook ISBN 978-1-61519-559-6

Cover design by Sarah Smith | Text design by Sarah Schneider
Cover photograph courtesy of Janice Milnerwood

Manufactured in the United States of America

First printing July 2019
10 9 8 7 6 5

CONTENTS

Introduction 1

1. What Is Baby-Led Weaning?

What Is Weaning? 7
Why BLW Is Different 8
Why BLW Makes Sense 10
When Should a Baby Start Solids? 11
Baby-Led Weaning Isn't New 13
A Brief History of Feeding Babies 16
What Your Mother Was Told 21
Building a Healthy Relationship with Food 25
The Trouble with Spoon-Feeding 27
The Benefits of BLW 34
Are There Any Disadvantages? 41

2. How Does Baby-Led Weaning Work?

Growing Skills 43
Self-Feeding: A Natural Skill 50
The Motivation to Try Solid Foods 50
Needing Extra Nutrients 51
The Importance of Milk Feedings 55
Developing the Ability to Chew 57

Is There Really a Window of Opportunity? 59
Eating Enough but Not Too Much:
Understanding Appetite Control 59
Won't He Choke? 61
Do Babies Really Know What They Need to Eat? 68
Baby-Led Weaning and Babies Born Preterm 70
Baby-Led Weaning in Special Cases 72

3. Getting Started
Preparing for BLW 77
When to Eat 79
Basic Safety 81
Finger Food 82
Improving Coordination 84
Offering Rather Than Giving 87
How Much Food to Offer 89
Rejecting Food 91
Helping Your Baby to Learn 92
Eating Together 97
Expect Mess 100
Equipment 103
The Secrets of Successful BLW 109
Q&A 110

4. First Foods
Basic Principles 117
Foods to Avoid 118
Foods That Are Different for Babies 124
What About Allergies? 126
Adapting Food in the Early Months 129
Drinks 138

Breakfast 140
Easy Snacks and Food on the Move 142
Desserts 143

5. After the Early Days
Progressing at Your Baby's Pace 147
Adventurous Taste Buds 150
Learning About Textures 153
Feast and Famine 156
Eating Enough: Learning to Trust Your Baby 158
Telling You She's Had Enough 161
Food Fads 163
Your Baby's Appetite for Milk Feedings 166
Three Meals a Day? 169
Your Baby's Diaper 172
Introducing a Cup 175
Introducing Cutlery 176
Eating Out 180
BLW and Childcare 185

6. A Healthy Diet for Everyone
Healthy Eating from the Start 191
Balancing Your Family's Diet 192
What We Need to Eat and Why 193
Variety Is the Spice of Life! 200
Buying Organic 202
Tips for Getting the Best Out of Your Food 203

7. Growing Up with BLW
Maintaining a Baby-Led Approach 207
Avoiding Negative Labels 208

Encouraging Self-Service 209
Mealtime Behavior 211
Bribes, Rewards, and Punishments 214
Avoiding an Emotional Battleground 215
Ending Milk Feedings 218

Conclusion *221*

Appendix 1: The Story of Baby-Led Weaning *223*
Appendix 2: Basic Rules for Food Safety *227*
References *231*
Photo Credits *232*
Acknowledgments *233*
Index *235*
About the Authors *242*

INTRODUCTION

The first time a baby eats solid food is a milestone for most parents—it's a new chapter in a baby's life and it's exciting. And as he takes his first mouthful of food, parents cross their fingers and hope that their baby will be a "good eater." They want him to enjoy food, to eat healthily, and they want to have easy, stress-free family mealtimes.

But many parents find the transition to solid food difficult for them and their child. They struggle with common problems, whether it's getting their baby to accept lumpy food or coping with picky eating or mealtime battles with a toddler. Often, families settle for separate mealtimes and different food for adults and children.

Most babies still start their journey to grown-up eating by being spoon-fed their first mouthfuls of puréed food on a date decided by their parents. But what happens if you don't do it like this? What happens if you let your baby decide when and how to start solids? What happens if you let him handle "real" food himself instead of spoon-feeding him? In other words, what happens if you let your baby lead the way?

Well, like increasing numbers of families, you and your baby will almost certainly find the whole adventure more fun. He'll show you when he's ready to start, and he'll share your meals from the very beginning. He'll learn about healthy family food by tasting and testing it and by feeding himself—no mush or purées but real food. And he'll be able to do all this from about six months and on.

Of course, there's nothing revolutionary about giving babies food they can hold from six months. What's different about baby-led weaning (BLW) is that the baby feeds himself *all* his food, making spoon-fed purées and "baby food" a thing of the past.

Baby-led weaning will develop your baby's chewing skills, manual dexterity, and hand-eye coordination. With your help, he'll discover a wide range of healthy foods and learn important social skills. And he'll eat only as much as he needs, making him less likely to be overweight when he is older. Most of all, he'll enjoy it—and he'll be happy and confident at mealtimes as a result.

Baby-led weaning is safe, natural, and easy—and, like most good ideas in parenting, it's not new; for generations, parents have discovered it for themselves, simply by watching their babies. Baby-led weaning works whether your baby is breast-fed, formula-fed, or both. And, according to parents who have tried both BLW and spoon-feeding, letting your baby lead the way is much easier and more enjoyable all around.

With BLW, there's no program to follow and no stages to complete. Your baby won't have to work his way through a series of smooth purées and mashed and lumpy meals before he's allowed to eat "real" food—and you won't have to follow a complicated daily timetable of meals. Instead, you'll be able to relax and enjoy your baby's adventures with food.

Most books on introducing solids (or "complementary foods") contain recipes and menu planners; this book is different. It's more about *how* to let your baby feed himself rather than just *what* to offer him. It will show you why BLW is the logical way to introduce solid foods and why trusting your baby's skills and instincts makes sense. It will provide you with practical tips for getting started and the lowdown on what to expect. In short, it will let you in on what has been one of the best-kept secrets of stress-free parenting.

Planning "baby meals" assumes that babies can't have ordinary family food or that their food has to be prepared separately. But as long as your own diet is healthy and nutritious, you'll find most meals can be adapted easily so that your six-month-old baby can share them. We have included some suggestions for good first foods and foods to avoid, to help you get started. If you need more inspiration or ideas for family mealtimes, take a look at *The Baby-Led Weaning Cookbook* or *The Baby-Led Weaning Cookbook—Volume 2.* Many parents see BLW as an opportunity to look at what *they* eat, too, so we've provided guidelines in this book on how to ensure a healthy and balanced diet for the whole family.

Baby-led weaning can be great fun for you as well as your baby. You'll probably be impressed at how quickly he becomes skilled at handling different foods and how adventurous he is with new tastes compared with other children. Babies are *happier* doing things for themselves, and it helps them learn.

Many parents who used a baby-led approach shared their experiences with us to help us write the original edition of this book, and this new edition includes further insights and real-life stories from families. Some had found spoon-feeding difficult in the past; others had turned to BLW in frustration when their six-month-old refused to be spoon-fed. Some were first-time parents who were attracted by BLW's reputation as a gentle and commonsense way to introduce solids. What we continue to hear is that their babies absolutely loved it and that they became—and remain—happy and sociable eaters.

In the years since this book was first published, BLW has had a growing impact on the way babies start complementary foods. Families all over the world have shown other parents, relatives, and health professionals that baby-led weaning simply makes sense. It has influenced guidelines for introducing complementary foods and inspired ongoing research in several countries. Spoon-feeding babies puréed foods seems increasingly to be an unnecessary, outdated idea.

We hope this fully revised and updated version of the classic baby-led weaning book will help you discover just how easy the transition to family meals can be and how using a baby-led approach can provide the foundation for a lifetime of healthy, enjoyable eating for your baby.

NOTE: Throughout this book, we've tried to be fair to boys and girls by alternating *he* and *she*, chapter by chapter. No difference between boys and girls is implied.

1 What Is Baby-Led Weaning?

"For most parents, mealtimes seem to be a nightmare. With Emily, that's one major battle we just don't have to face. We really enjoy mealtimes. Food is not an issue at all."

Jess, mother of Emily, 2 years

"It's so much easier to introduce the same food that everyone else is eating. I just don't worry about whether or not Ben will eat something the way I did with the others when I was spoon-feeding. This feels so natural—and so much more enjoyable."

Sam, mother of Bella, 8 years;
Alex, 5 years; and Ben, 8 months

What Is Weaning?

Weaning is the gradual change that a baby makes from having breast milk or formula as her only food to having no breast milk or formula at all. This changeover takes *at least* six months but may—especially with breastfeeding—last several years. This book is mostly about the beginning of the weaning process, which starts with the baby's very first mouthful of solid food.*

The first solids—also called complementary foods—are not meant to replace breast milk or formula but to add to (or "complement") it, so that the baby's diet gradually becomes more varied.

In most families, weaning is led by the parents. When they start to spoon-feed their baby, they are deciding when and how she starts solids; when they stop offering the breast or bottle, they are deciding when to end milk feedings. You could call it parent-led weaning. Baby-led weaning (BLW) is different. It allows the baby to lead the whole process, using her instincts and abilities. She determines when weaning should start and finish. This makes perfect sense when you look closely at how babies develop.

Why BLW Is Different

When people think about introducing a baby's first solid foods, they usually picture an adult with a spoon and some puréed carrot or apple. Sometimes, the baby will open her mouth eagerly to take the spoon—but she is just as likely to spit the food out, push the spoon away, cry, or refuse to eat. Many parents resort to games—"Here comes the train!"—in an effort to persuade the baby to accept food, which is often different from the family's meals and given at a different time.

---

* Throughout this book, *weaning* refers to the introduction of solid foods. However, the term *weaning* can also be used to describe the transition from breast milk to formula. For this reason, baby-led weaning is sometimes also called "baby-led solids."

Until recent years, this approach to feeding babies has rarely been questioned. Most people take it for granted that spoon-feeding is the normal way to go about introducing complementary foods. And yet dictionary definitions for spoon-feeding include "to provide (someone) with so much help or information that they do not need to think for themselves"[1] and "to treat (another) in a way that discourages independent thought or action."[2] Baby-led weaning, on the other hand, encourages a baby's confidence and independence by following *her* cues. Eating solid foods starts when the baby begins to feed herself and progresses at her unique pace. It allows her to follow her instincts to copy her parents and her siblings and to develop her feeding skills in a natural, fun way, learning as she goes.

If they are given the chance, almost all babies will show their parents that they are ready for something other than milk simply by grabbing a piece of food and bringing it to their mouths. They don't need their parents to decide when complementary feeding should start, and they don't need to be spoon-fed; babies can do it themselves.

This is what happens in BLW:

- The baby sits with the rest of the family at mealtimes and joins in when she is ready.
- She is encouraged to explore food as soon as she is interested, by picking it up with her hands—it doesn't matter whether or not she eats any.
- Food is offered in pieces that are the size and shape that the baby can handle easily, rather than as purées or mashed food.

- She feeds herself from the start, rather than being spoon-fed by someone else.
- It's up to the baby how much she eats and how quickly she widens the range of foods she enjoys.
- The baby continues to have milk feedings (breast milk or formula) whenever she wants them, and she decides when she is ready to begin reducing them.

The first experiences of eating solid food can have an impact on the way a baby feels about mealtimes for many years, so it makes sense to make them enjoyable. But for many babies—and their parents—starting solid food isn't much fun. Of course, not all babies mind being spoon-fed in the conventional way, but many appear to resign themselves to it rather than truly enjoy it. On the other hand, babies who are allowed to feed themselves and eat with the family seem to love mealtimes.

> "When Ryan was about six months, I went out with a group of moms with babies the same age. The mothers were busy spooning purée into their babies and wiping around their mouths with the spoon, making sure every bit went in. They seemed to be making their lives so hard, and you could see the babies weren't enjoying it."
>
> Suzanne, mother of Ryan, 2 years

Why BLW Makes Sense

Babies and children crawl, walk, and talk when they are ready. These developmental milestones won't happen any sooner and—provided babies are given the opportunity—they won't happen any later than the right time for that baby. When you put your newborn baby on the floor to kick her legs, you are giving her the opportunity to roll over. When she can, she will. You're also providing her with the opportunity to get up and walk. That may take a bit longer. But keep on providing the opportunity and she will do it eventually. Why should feeding be any different?

Most healthy babies are able to feed themselves from their mother's breast as soon as they are born. By the time they are about six months old, they are able to reach out and grab pieces of food and bring them to their mouth. We've always known that they can do this, and, for many years, parents have been encouraged to introduce finger foods from about six months. But there has been evidence for some time to show that babies shouldn't be having *any* solids before this age (see the next section). Since babies can begin to feed themselves with finger foods starting at six months, there seems to be no need for puréed foods at all.

However, even though we now know that babies have both the instinct and the ability to feed themselves at the right time, spoon-feeding is still the way most babies are fed during their first year, and sometimes for much longer.

When Should a Baby Start Solids?

Since 2002, the World Health Organization (and many other authorities, such as Health Canada and the UK Departments of Health) have recommended that all babies should, if possible, have nothing but breast milk until they are six months old and that complementary foods should be introduced gradually from then on.[3] This recommendation has since been adopted by the American Academy of Pediatrics. Evidence suggests that giving solid foods earlier than six months is not good for babies because of the following reasons:

- Solid foods are not as densely packed with nutrients and calories as breast milk or formula. Young babies have small tummies and need a concentrated, easily digestible source of calories and nutrients for healthy growth; only breast milk or formula can provide this.
- The baby's digestive system isn't able to get all the goodness out of solid foods, so they pass through her without giving her proper nourishment.
- If she has solid foods too early, the baby's appetite for breast milk or formula goes down, so she gets even less nourishment.
- Babies who are given solid foods early are more prone to infections than those who stay on breast milk or formula until six months, because until this age their immune system is immature.

Feeding babies solid foods earlier than six months has also been found to make them more prone to risk factors for heart disease in later life, such as high blood pressure.

Why is some baby food labeled as suitable from four months?

The World Health Organization's code of conduct, the *International Code of Marketing of Breast-Milk Substitutes*, restricts the promotion of any foods or drinks for babies under six months old, and almost all countries of the world have signed on to it. But in many countries, including the USA and the UK, much of the *International Code* remains voluntary—in other words, it doesn't *have* to be followed by the food industry. Because manufacturers of baby food want to maximize their sales, many choose to use labeling that implies that their products are appropriate for babies younger than six months, even though this isn't true. So, until the law is changed, some baby food will continue to be labeled as suitable "from four months."

Baby-Led Weaning Isn't New

Although the name is fairly new, baby-led weaning is probably as old as humankind. For generations, parents, especially those who have three or more children, have discovered that letting the baby take the lead makes life easier and more enjoyable for everyone. Mostly, their story goes something like this: They did as they were told with their first baby, finding that introducing solids required a lot of patience. They relaxed a bit with the second child, breaking some of the rules, and discovered that moving on to family meals was a bit easier as a result. By the time their third baby was born, they were so busy they just "let her get on with it."

These parents often say that their first child—spoon-fed according to all the guidelines—turned into quite a fussy eater. The second baby was probably a bit less picky, but the third baby became a noticeably "better" eater than the other two—less fussy and more adventurous. The parents had discovered BLW. Unfortunately, because they were worried that they would be thought bad parents—or even just plain lazy—they didn't tell anyone.

BLW STORY

When I first started baby-led weaning with Miguel, my Brazilian grandma told me that's how she'd introduced solids with her own children—she let them feed themselves. She started to cry when she saw him with food, she was so emotional! Then she told me that when I was a baby and my parents started me on solid foods, they wanted to spoon-feed me and it caused arguments between them all. My grandma couldn't understand what they were doing, and my parents told her she was living in the past. So she was really happy when she saw me doing BLW. But my mom thought I was just doing it to be different. After a few months she could see how Miguel was growing into a confident, capable, happy eater and how much he liked fruits and vegetables, so when Alice started two years later, she was expecting we would do BLW again and didn't make any effort to change our minds.

My grandma told me I was right to let Miguel feed himself and said she'd been taught that children must eat with the family, all together. She said they didn't have high chairs in those days but used to have a wooden box next to the table, where they'd sit the baby so he could eat without falling. Listening to her stories gave me so much confidence—I knew that it was natural and safe.

A few months after Miguel started BLW, I asked my husband's grandma, who is Japanese, what she did. She said she was taught to start solids by letting the baby feed himself, too! She said there was a saying: "When baby sits, baby eats." Both grandmas said they couldn't remember any official advice from doctors; all the wisdom was passed from mother to daughter, grandmother to granddaughter. They told us that every baby grows in their own time, so parents must watch each one and wait until they can sit up. They both said we should offer plain foods, avoid hard foods, and let them try to pick it up themselves to eat. It seemed really simple. Neither of them knew it as baby-led weaning, but really this has been part of my family for years.

Melina, mother of Miguel, 5 years; Alice, 3 years; and Cecília, 1 year

"The more people I talk to, the more I realize that introducing solids this way is not a new idea. So many people say: 'Actually, I did that, I just didn't talk about it.' Parents have been doing this for years—it just didn't have a name." Clare, mother of Louise, 7 months

A Brief History of Feeding Babies

Historically, not a great deal is known about how babies in the UK and North America were introduced to solid foods much before the late nineteenth century; parenting skills and knowledge were passed from mother to daughter, with very little written down. But it is likely that, as today, many families discovered BLW for themselves. And although anecdotal evidence suggests that, throughout the twentieth century at least some families introduced solids this way, the story was very different for most babies.

At the beginning of the twentieth century, babies didn't have any solid foods until they were eight or nine months, or even older. Although hard-baked biscuits or crusts would sometimes be given from around seven months, these were intended only as a way of developing chewing skills or to help with teething, not as food. By the 1960s, the age for the introduction of solid foods had dropped to as early as two or three months. It then rose slightly, so that by the 1990s most babies were having solids from around four months old. Most of these changes came about because of changes in the advice mothers were given about breastfeeding; there was little sound research into infant feeding and, for a long time, no official guidelines on introducing solids.

In the early 1900s, almost all babies were breastfed—either by their own mother or by a wet nurse (a woman employed by parents to breastfeed their baby). As wet-nursing became less popular and birth became more medicalized, doctors started to see it as their role to advise mothers on how to breastfeed their own babies. Leaving things to the instinct of the mother—or even worse, her baby—was thought to be unreliable, and feeding began to be carefully controlled from the day the baby was born.

> "My grandma thought it was great when she saw Rosy feeding herself. She was the eldest of seven children and she said that was the way she remembered her mother feeding her younger brothers and sisters. She couldn't remember any spoon-feeding at all. She said she'd only spoon-fed my mom because she was told to start at three months."
>
> Linda, mother of Rosy, 22 months

Although breastfeeding was recognized as the best way to feed babies, the fact that they needed to feed frequently for their mothers to make enough milk wasn't understood. Mothers were told to follow a strict timetable, limiting the time the baby spent at the breast and spacing feeds several hours apart. As a result, many quickly found their supply diminishing. No surprise, then, that the few substitute formulas available at the time began to grow in popularity and to be recommended by doctors, in an effort to make sure babies got the nourishment they needed.

As restricted, "by the clock" feeding became more widespread and more mothers turned to the new infant formulas, it became clear that these products weren't as good for babies as their advertisements suggested. Babies fed on these milks frequently got sick or were undernourished, and the feedings were often complicated to prepare, so mistakes were common.

Since most mothers still preferred to start their babies on the breast, even if (because of the regimented feeding schedules) they were only able to feed them for a few months, doctors—and the authors of the newly popular "mothercraft" books—saw the answer as encouraging breastfeeding from birth but introducing solid foods as soon as it was clear that the mother was no longer producing enough breast milk, usually when the baby was between two and four months of age. Chubbiness was seen as a sign of good health, so mothers were encouraged to give their babies cereal as a first food, to ensure they gained plenty of weight.

At around the same time, preprepared "strained" foods began appearing in stores, and, by the 1930s, a variety of fruit- and vegetable-based baby food was available. These were intended for older babies, but it was found that they could just as easily be fed to very young babies.

Once babies were routinely being given solid foods from before the age they could chew, the practice of introducing teething biscuits declined. And, although the need to introduce foods that were closer to family meals was still acknowledged, babies usually progressed to lumpy foods given by spoon rather than being given foods that they could hold.

In the 1960s, it was recognized that babies needed to practice chewing food and moving it around their mouths, and parents were encouraged to introduce finger foods from around six months. However, because it was assumed that babies needed to get used to very soft foods before they could learn to chew, most people believed they had to start purées *before* six months in order to be able to move on to chewable foods at the right time.

When the American Academy of Pediatrics' guidelines were issued in 1980, most babies of three months were already having something other than milk feedings (usually baby cereal). The guidelines said that babies shouldn't be given any solid foods until they were at least four months old and that they should all be having some other foods by the time they reached six months. This advice has now been updated in line with the World Health Organization's 2002 recommendation of exclusive breastfeeding (or formula-feeding) until six months.

Is BLW recommended?

In recent years, enthusiasm for BLW has spread rapidly among families and it is actively supported by many health care professionals. Even though it isn't always mentioned by name, many of the principles of BLW, such as shared mealtimes, allowing babies to handle food from the start, and the need to respect babies' appetites, are now firmly embedded in infant-feeding guidelines around the world. Many now suggest that first foods can be either offered as pieces the baby can hold or puréed and fed by spoon.

Along with this rise in popularity, there's been a growing focus on BLW among researchers interested in infant feeding. While there is more to be learned, it is becoming clear that BLW is indeed a safe approach to starting solids and that it may have positive implications for babies' long-term health and development as well as for their relationship with food.[4] As the body of evidence grows, it's quite possible the expectation that babies will be spoon-fed will become a thing of the past.

BLW STORY

When I had my daughter, I instinctively decided I wasn't going to do solids until she was ready. I'd had such a miserable experience with my first child, Jack, trying to start him on solids at four months. But that was the guidance at the time. Now, of course, I realize that he wasn't developmentally or psychologically up to it. He hated it. Anna was perfectly happy just breastfeeding, so I just didn't bother with purées at all. We didn't go to the doctor's very much, but if they asked me, I just lied. I remember her eight-month checkup, and I said: "Yes, she's on three meals a day, she's loving it," when in reality, she'd only helped herself to a few bits and pieces of food that the rest of us were eating. She went straight from breast milk to picking up food and eating it. There were no stages: no fine purée, then mash, then lumps. At that time most babies would have been on three full meals by the time they were six months. People who knew I wasn't spoon-feeding her were confused, but they could see that she was fine. They probably just thought I was lazy. And when Anna did start eating, when she was a bit over eight months, everyone could see she was managing normal food perfectly well and that she was quite happy.

Lizzie, mother of three grown children

What Your Mother Was Told

If you were born in the 1970s, '80s, or '90s, your parents would have been given advice by health professionals about when and how to introduce solid foods. This was based on the limited research available at that time, which was very different from the evidence-based information we have today. However, some of this old advice has persisted and, like your parents, you may be encouraged to look for specific signs, such as those listed below, to help you judge your baby's "readiness." The problem is that most of these signs simply reflect the normal development and behavior of babies from three to four months old. They are not related to the need for other foods or to the ability to digest them, so they *don't* indicate readiness for solids.

False signs of readiness for solid food

- *Waking at night.* Babies wake at night for all sorts of reasons, and there is no evidence that giving them solid food solves the problem. If they *are* genuinely hungry, babies under six months need to be offered more breast milk (or formula, if they are formula-fed), not solids.
- *Weight gain slowing slightly.* Research has shown this is something that normally happens at around four months, especially in breastfed babies. It's not a sign that they need solid food.
- *Watching their parents eat.* From about four months babies are fascinated by everyday family activities, such as dressing, shaving, cleaning teeth—and eating. But they

don't understand what these things mean; they're just curious.

- *Disappearance of the "tongue thrust."* At around four months, this reflex, which pushes anything solid out of the mouth, starts to disappear (see page 58). While this may make spoon-feeding easier, it isn't a sign that the baby is ready to digest solid foods.
- *Small baby.* If a small baby is undernourished (rather than being genetically destined to be small), she needs nutrient-rich breast milk or formula to help her grow, not solids. (Babies born preterm may have different needs; see pages 70–71.)
- *Big baby.* A big baby's size may be due to her genetic makeup, or, if she is formula-fed, it may be because she is having more milk than she needs. Her digestive and immune systems are no more ready for solids than any other baby's. (The link between weight and starting solids dates from the 1950s, when it was believed babies needed solid food when they doubled their birth weight or reached 12 pounds [5.5 kilograms], whichever came sooner.)

> **"I've never understood why people say: 'Oh, he's big; he needs more; you should give him solids,' because the food most people start with—pear, apple, or steamed carrot—those are things you would eat if you were going on a diet."**
>
> Holly, mother of Ava, 7 years;
> Archie, 4 years; and Glen, 6 months

BLW STORY

Max has always been big for his age, 98th percentile. So, I was always hearing from people about big babies, how they would be getting extra hungry and need solids from four months and so on. But I just let myself be guided by him. And despite being a big baby, he didn't seem to really get into food. I could tell from his diapers that he was probably eating something from about eight months, but I don't think he was eating lots until about ten months. I really saw the first six months of BLW as just being for him to explore tastes and textures, so I didn't worry about the fact that, compared to my friends who were feeding purées, I couldn't really tell how much he was eating. I think feeding this way took the pressure off, really. I'd tried spoon-feeding my nephews, and there was a certain amount they were supposed to eat from the jar, and I found it very stressful when they just decided to stop. With BLW you have to be a bit relaxed about it, initially, and let them take it at their own pace. It's quite easy to just assume they're not eating anything, and that they're going to be starving, and that you need to feed them something. I used to think: "Why am I worrying? Breast milk is much more nutritious for him than half a carrot." I assumed that he was getting whatever nutrition he needed from the breast milk. And breastfeeding fit in so easily around mealtimes. He just fed whenever he wanted to and it just all came together.

Charlotte, mother of Max, 16 months

In a similar way, the old advice about *how* to introduce solid foods simply reflected the fact that babies of four months are not capable of feeding themselves or chewing. Because their oral development and digestive and immune systems are so immature at that age, it was important to stress the need for carefully controlled stages, plain foods, and getting used to the spoon. So your first experience of solid food may well have been cereal, made into a smooth, almost runny purée, given by spoon. You would have progressed to one meal a day of puréed fruit or vegetables, with three days' gap before each new food was introduced (in case you had a bad reaction). By six months, you would have been on three meals a day, at which point you would have been introduced to foods with lumps and to finger foods. You probably wouldn't have been allowed to play with your food, because that was considered bad. The aim over the first year would have been to replace milk feedings with solid meals as quickly as possible and to stop breast milk or formula completely by your first birthday.

Of course, we now understand that babies' digestive and immune systems are simply not ready for anything other than breast milk or formula at four months and that breast milk is important for babies for at least the first two years. So it's clear that the introduction of solid foods should be approached in a very different way, starting when babies are developmentally ready. And, as we'll see in Chapter 2, the best sign that a baby is ready is when she starts to put food into her mouth herself—which she can only do if she is given the opportunity.

"When the child on your lap grabs a handful of your dinner from your plate, chews it, and swallows it, then it might be time to push the plate nearer to her."

Gabrielle Palmer, nutritionist and author

Building a Healthy Relationship with Food

Experiences with food in the first years of a child's life can affect her behavior and attitudes around food for a lifetime. If you think about your own relationship with food, as an adult, chances are some elements relate back to your childhood, a time when emotions and food can easily become tangled up together. Maybe you were given food as a reward for being good or for eating a food you didn't like. Or maybe you were just persuaded to ignore your body's signs of fullness and eat "one more spoonful for Grandma" or to clear your plate. Adults eat for all sorts of reasons, not just because they need nutrients or feel hungry. They eat out of habit, because the clock says it's dinnertime or because others are eating around them. They might eat before going out to keep themselves from getting hungry later. Many people eat certain foods to comfort themselves when they are feeling down or bored, or to reward themselves. Sometimes people eat to please someone else or just to prevent food going to waste. Many of these habits are learned in the very early childhood years, and they can lead to a distorted relationship with food that is lifelong. Baby-led weaning avoids all of this and allows babies to tune into their bodies, so that they develop a healthy relationship with food from the outset.

BLW STORY

I have a terrible relationship with food that I don't want my daughter, Elinor, to repeat. Hopefully, if she is in control of what she eats from the start, then the dinner table won't become a battleground for her the way it was for me.

As a toddler I had to sit at the table until I had finished all my food, and I often used to gag and vomit the food back up. But it was a power struggle I always won because no one can really make you eat. Even now I eat "like a child" and gag on lots of flavors and textures.

To be honest, as Elinor approached six months, the thought of having to cook (and taste) those awful-smelling purées was really making me dread starting solids with her. If *I* didn't want to eat them, why on earth would she? My public health nurse was great—she was really happy when I mentioned BLW. I later found out she had done something similar with her own children, years ago.

Now that I have to set a good example with food, it's actually forcing me to eat better myself. I used to just eat things like canned spaghetti, but I want Elinor to see me eating healthy foods. There's more healthy stuff in the fridge nowadays, and it's having a really positive impact on our diet.

Jackie, mother of Elinor, 7 months

The Trouble with Spoon-Feeding

Imagine you are six months old. You enjoy copying whatever you see your family doing, and you want to grab the things they are handling to find out what they are. As you watch your parents eating, you're fascinated by the smells, shapes, and colors. You don't understand that they are eating because they're hungry; you simply want to try whatever it is they're doing—that's how you learn. But instead of allowing you to join in, your parents put something mushy into your mouth with a spoon. The mush is always the same consistency, but the taste seems to vary: Sometimes it's nice; sometimes it's not. Your parents might let you see it, but they rarely let you touch it. At times they seem to be in a hurry; at other times you have to wait for the next mouthful. When you spit the food out because you weren't expecting it (or even just to see what it looks like), they scrape it up and poke it back in again! You haven't yet learned that this mush can fill your tummy, so if you're hungry you'll probably feel frustrated because what you want is a milk feeding. Maybe if you're not too hungry and the mush tastes nice, you'll go along with it. But you are still curious about what everyone else is doing and would rather be allowed to do the same.

Spoon-feeding isn't exactly *bad*—it's simply not necessary.[5] And, while many babies who are spoon-fed go on to enjoy mealtimes without any problems, feeding babies this way carries a potential for creating problems, which doesn't exist with BLW. Partly this has to do with the consistency of puréed or mashed food, and partly it's to do with how much control the baby has over her eating:

- Many spoon-fed babies gag on lumpy or mashed foods when they are first introduced. This is because when they suck them off the spoon to the back of their mouth, they trigger their gag reflex (see pages 62–64). It is more difficult for a baby to work out how to avoid gagging when she is spoon-fed than when she is putting the food into her mouth herself, and many babies simply decide to refuse the spoon.
- Being spoon-fed by someone else means the baby is not in control of how much she eats or how fast. Sloppy food gets swallowed quickly, and it's tempting to persuade the baby to have "just one more spoonful." Often, babies eat faster than they would do otherwise and end up having more than they really need. Even when a parent is particularly responsive to their child and stops offering food when she turns her head away, the chances are the baby will already have eaten all she needed a few spoonfuls earlier. Persistently persuading a child to eat more than she needs interferes with her ability to sense when she is full and could lead to a lifelong problem with overeating.
- Milk feedings are the most important source of nourishment for a baby under a year old. Solids are less nutrient-rich than either breast milk or formula. If a baby is given too much solid food, her appetite for breast milk or formula will be reduced. As a result, she may get less of some nutrients than she needs.
- Spoon-feeding is simply not as much fun for the baby as self-feeding. Babies want to explore food, because that's how they learn. They don't generally like having

things done to them or for them. Allowing babies to feed themselves makes mealtimes more enjoyable and encourages them to trust food, making it more likely that they will enjoy a wide range of tastes and textures.

This doesn't mean BLW babies can never have mushy foods or that they will never learn to use a spoon. Babies have a sharp instinct to copy those around them, so if you and your family use cutlery, your baby will want to try it out as well. A few babies manage to feed themselves with a preloaded spoon early on, others learn to "dip" spoons fairly quickly, and, as we'll see, there are many other ways babies can manage sloppy foods. The problem isn't the spoon itself—it's who's controlling it.

Being in control of what she eats allows your baby to taste new foods at the front of her mouth and spit them out if she doesn't like them. A spoonful of puréed food is much more difficult to dislodge, so, unless she's sure it's something she likes, the baby may refuse it. It's easy to see how this can lead to babies refusing all but their favorite flavors.

> "Mealtimes became like a battleground for a couple of weeks when I was giving Mabel purées; she wouldn't even try anything off the spoon. I found it so frustrating. I don't know if it was the spoon issue, or the texture of the purée, or a combination of both. But the minute I gave her something that she could feed herself and that she was in control of, mealtimes were fun for her and she would try anything. She wouldn't touch puréed corn, but when I gave her those little baby corns, she couldn't get enough of them."
>
> Becky, mother of Mabel, 10 months

> "When I was spoon-feeding Ivan, I'd have to trick him into laughing to get the spoon into his mouth, but it would just come straight back out. So I'd just get it in from any angle I could before he turned his head away. He obviously didn't want it, but we were convinced he needed the food. So we would sit there, getting frustrated, watching the clock ticking while we tried to get the whole jar into him. Looking back, I can see he probably didn't need it."
>
> Pam, mother of Ivan, 3 years; and Molly, 18 months

Learning to eat from a spoon held by someone else isn't (as used to be thought) a vital stage in the development of eating skills. Indeed, throughout much of human existence, spoons were relatively unknown. Some cultures have long believed that it's important to touch and feel food to really enjoy it and that using any sort of cutlery spoils the experience; others simply don't see the need to use tools to eat. And yet, in most Western countries, it has been assumed for many years that you just can't get food into a baby without using a spoon.

Of course, spoon-feeding seemed logical when it was believed that babies of three or four months needed solid foods since, at that age, they couldn't chew food or get it to their mouth themselves. This led to an assumption that purées and spoon-feeding were an essential part of introducing solids. But there doesn't appear to have been any research to back this up. Even in recent times, most research into complementary feeding has focused on what to give babies and when, rather than how. As a result, the relationship between the normal development of babies and how they are introduced to solids has been largely overlooked. In fact, until recently nobody seems to have investigated whether spoon-feeding is either safe or appropriate for babies—it has simply become common practice: "tried and trusted," but not actually tested.

The trouble with purées

Puréed foods are, of course, helpful for people who have difficulty chewing, but most babies of six months don't need to have their food puréed for them any more than most adults do.[6] Some mashed or puréed foods are part of most family diets (thick soups, soft mashed potatoes, etc.), but there are problems with presenting babies with *all* their food this way:

- The consistency of puréed or mashed food means that it is easy to suck it off a spoon; it doesn't need to be chewed. If a baby doesn't get the chance to experiment with food that needs chewing soon after she reaches six months, the development of chewing skills can be delayed. Babies who aren't introduced to pieces of food until they are almost a year old (or later) may never learn to manage lumps well. It's the equivalent of not giving a child the chance to walk until they're, say, three years old. Chewing skills are important for many reasons, including the development of safe eating (see pages 57–58).
- Babies learn to cope with lumps better and more quickly if they can feed themselves, because it's easier to manipulate and chew food when it starts off at the front of the mouth. Foods fed by spoon tend to be sucked straight to the back of the mouth where they can't be moved around as easily or safely.

- Our mouths are designed to mash food by chewing. Food that is thoroughly chewed is easier for the stomach to deal with than food that has been swallowed quickly (as purées tend to be) because mixing it with saliva helps to kick-start the digestive process, especially the digestion of starchy foods. Babies who are offered pieces of food and allowed to eat at their own pace tend to chew for a long time before they swallow, facilitating good digestion.
- Puréeing food—especially fruit and vegetables—can affect its nutritional value. When food is cut up, some of the vitamin C is lost from the exposed surfaces. Puréeing increases this loss, so food that is puréed in advance will be lower in vitamin C than it would have been if it had been eaten in large pieces. A whole banana, for example, will provide more vitamin C than the same banana puréed or mashed. Vitamin C is an important nutrient, especially as it encourages the absorption of iron. And the body isn't able to store vitamin C, so it's important to have a good source every day.
- Puréeing, like juicing, releases sugars from within the food, converting them into "free sugars" that are available before the food is swallowed. This poses risks for tooth decay as well as making the food taste sweeter, encouraging a liking for extra-sweet flavors.

> **"I try to spoon-feed Sammy when we are out so it's less messy, but he's not happy with it. He doesn't make a fuss, but he usually just spits the food out, looks at it, then picks it up and eats it from his fingers."**
>
> Claire, mother of Sammy, 10 months

BLW: A different eating experience

The BLW experience is very different for your baby from the conventional spoon-feeding approach. If you were six months old, which would you choose?

THE BABY-LED APPROACH	THE CONVENTIONAL APPROACH
Baby is given the opportunity to eat	Baby is expected to eat
Mealtimes are shared	Baby often eats separately
Baby has the same food as everyone else	Baby's food looks different (even if it has the same ingredients)
Baby can touch and pick up the food	Food is usually kept out of reach
Baby is exposed to lots of different shapes, colors, textures, and tastes	Baby's food has a limited range of shapes, colors, textures, and tastes
Baby chooses when to broaden her range of textures; progress is gradual and self-directed	New textures are introduced in stages; progress is decided by the parent
Baby gets to choose each mouthful	Mouthfuls are chosen by the parent (and may be unexpected)
Baby chooses the pace of the meal	Pace is decided by the parent
Baby decides how much to eat	Parent decides how much baby should eat
Baby is active: touching and exploring	Baby is passive (unless refusing to eat)
Baby decides when to start cutting down intake of breast milk or formula and when to stop breastfeeding completely	Baby's intake of breast milk or formula is largely determined by the amount of food she is encouraged to eat

Why not a bit of both?

Parents are sometimes encouraged (by health professionals, or by books on introducing solid foods) to do a "bit of both," that is, to combine spoon-feeding with elements of BLW. Typically, they let the baby feed herself for most of the meal and then give her a few spoonfuls at the end, just to make sure she's had enough. However, this combined approach is really no different from conventional weaning, which has always incorporated some finger foods from around six months alongside spoon-feeding.

Baby-led weaning isn't just about self-feeding; it's about letting the baby lead the way through the *whole* transition from breast- or formula-feeding to family food. It's about trusting her to know what, and how much, she needs to eat at every meal, not just sometimes. As soon as these decisions are taken over by an adult, according to their idea of what the baby should eat, it's no longer baby-led. And it means that many of the benefits of BLW (see below) are lost. It's simply not possible to combine an approach that revolves around complete trust for the baby with one in which the parent has the final say.

The Benefits of BLW

It's enjoyable!

Eating should be pleasurable for everyone—adults and babies alike. Playing an active part in mealtimes and being in control of what to eat, how much to eat, and how fast to eat it make eating more enjoyable. On the contrary, the opposite can make mealtimes miserable and may even lead to eating disorders later in life. If a baby's early experiences with food are healthy and happy, problems such as food refusal and food phobias are much less likely.

Being part of family mealtimes

Babies are included in family mealtimes from the start, eating the same food and joining in the social time. This is fun for the baby and allows her to copy mealtime behavior so that she will naturally move on to using cutlery and adopt the table manners expected in her family. Babies learn how different foods are eaten and how to share, wait their turn, and make conversation.

Sharing mealtimes has a positive impact on family relationships, social skills, language development, and healthy eating. When babies are fed separately from the rest of the family, keeping them amused while everyone else eats can be a challenge. With BLW, everyone eats together, so everyone is part of what's going on.

Learning about real food

Babies who are allowed to feed themselves learn about the look, smell, taste, and texture of different foods and how different flavors work together. With spoon-feeding it's common for several tastes to be puréed into one. BLW babies can discover the different tastes in, say, a chicken and vegetable casserole and begin to recognize foods they like. And they can simply leave anything they don't like rather than having to refuse the whole casserole to avoid it. It also means that the whole family can share a meal, even if not everyone likes all the flavors.

Learning to trust food

Because BLW babies are allowed to use their instincts to decide what to eat and what to leave, as toddlers they rarely show any suspicion of food. Allowing them to reject a food they feel they don't need or that may seem unsafe (over- or underripe, rancid, or poisonous) means babies are more willing to try new foods because they know they'll be allowed to decide whether or not to eat them.

> **"To start with, Emma was much more interested in food when she could see what it was. She was a bit more cautious with anything that was mixed together, even stews. She'd still eat it, but she'd spend a bit of time examining it first, as if she needed to check it out."**
>
> Michelle, mother of Emma, 2 years

Learning to eat safely

With BLW, babies have the chance to explore food before they put it in their mouth. They also get to practice chewing and moving food around inside their mouth so they become skilled at dealing with food more quickly than babies who are only spoon-fed. Learning to chew effectively is part of making eating safer and is also good for speech and digestion.

Better nutrition

Available evidence suggests that children whose parents adopt BLW and involve them in their mealtimes from the beginning are less likely to choose unhealthy foods when they are older and are therefore more likely to be better nourished in the long term. This may be because they are used to copying what their parents do and to eating adult food wherever they are, or because they tend to be more adventurous eaters anyway. It could also be because baby-led weaning doesn't teach them to see unhealthy foods as more desirable.

Having the opportunity to deal with a broad range of foods from the beginning means mealtimes are more interesting for the baby and makes it more likely that she will get all the nutrients she needs. And, because milk feedings are reduced very gradually, BLW babies who are breastfed are more likely to continue getting a good intake of breast milk for longer. Breastfeeding provides not only a perfect balance of nutrients but also protection, for both children and their mothers, against many serious illnesses.

Appetite control

Eating habits developed during childhood can last a lifetime. Research has shown that BLW babies have "greater satiety awareness," so it seems likely that babies who are allowed to choose what to eat from a range of nutritious foods, at their own pace, and to decide when they've had enough continue to eat according to their appetite and may be less likely to overeat when they are older.[7]

Making scientific discoveries

Babies are programmed to experiment and explore. They use their hands and mouths to find out about all sorts of objects, including food. Pretty much everything babies can learn from the best (and most expensive) educational toy can be learned by handling food. For instance, when something falls from their grasp, they find out about gravity. They learn about concepts such as less and more, size, shape, weight, and texture, too. Because all their senses (sight, touch, hearing, smell, and taste) are involved, they discover how to relate all these things together for a better understanding of the world around them.

Improving dexterity and coordination

By feeding themselves, babies can practice important aspects of their development at every mealtime. Using their fingers to get food to their mouths develops their hand-eye coordination, while gripping foods of different sizes and textures several times a day improves their dexterity. They work out how to hold something soft without squashing it or something slippery without dropping it. All this may help with skills such as writing and drawing later on.

> **"Everyone says Emmanuel's skills with his hands are amazing for his age, but I think it's normal. Every baby should be able to do those things; it's just that they don't get the opportunity to practice the way they do if they are feeding themselves a variety of foods every day. But nobody believes me when I say it's because he's always fed himself."** Antonietta, mother of Emmanuel, 2 years

Gaining confidence

Allowing babies to do things for themselves not only enables them to learn but also gives them confidence in their own abilities and judgment. When a baby picks something up and gets it to her mouth, she receives an almost instant reward in the form of an interesting taste or texture. This teaches her that she is capable of making good things happen, which in turn helps to build her confidence and self-esteem. As her experience of food grows, and she discovers what's edible and what isn't, and what to expect from each type of food, she learns to trust her own judgment. Many parents find that seeing their child feed herself helps them to trust her to explore and experiment in other areas of her life.

> **"The first time I saw a BLW baby eat, I was really struck by how confident she was with ordinary adult foods. At ten months, she was picking out pieces of food to eat, and she obviously knew what the different foods were and was used to choosing what she wanted. She seemed so content—and she was thoroughly enjoying her meal."**
>
> Maryanne, day care manager

Easier (and cheaper) meals

Letting the baby share what's being cooked for the rest of the family is cheaper than buying and preparing separate meals, and it's much less time-consuming and fussy. With BLW, provided your diet is healthy, you can easily adapt meals for your baby. And rather than having separate mealtimes or spoon-feeding her while your own dinner goes cold, you and your baby get to eat together.

Less pickiness and fewer battles

Pickiness and food refusal are less likely with BLW. This is because eating is enjoyable with this approach and, since the baby is eating normal family foods from the start, there isn't the transition from baby foods to lumpier meals and then to family meals, which many babies find difficult.

Because BLW respects babies' decisions about what to eat (or not to eat) and when to stop eating, there is no call for elaborate games involving train and airplane noises to try to fool a baby into accepting food she doesn't want. And there is no need to trick toddlers into eating healthily by making food into special shapes (such as smiley faces) or hiding vegetables in other dishes.

When there is no pressure on babies to eat, there is no opportunity for mealtimes to become a battleground. Instead, the whole family can enjoy stress-free meals together.

> **"I find that babies who have been encouraged to have solids this way enjoy a more varied diet and seem to be less fussy with foods later on."**
>
> Beverley, public health nurse

Eating out is easier

Baby-led weaning makes eating out simple. There are no concerns about preparing puréed food in advance or heating up the food while you are out. And there is usually something on the restaurant menu that a BLW baby can share and enjoy.

> **"I can't believe how easy it is when we go out. My granddaughter just eats what we eat. When my son was her age I always had to take jars or packets and find a way of heating it up. She tries everything we give her and has a great variety. It seems far less hassle than in my day!"**
>
> Anne, grandmother of Lilly, 9 months

Are There Any Disadvantages?

The mess

OK, yes, it *is* a bit messy! But all babies need to learn to feed themselves at some point, and that will involve some mess. It's just that, with BLW, the mess comes earlier than it would otherwise. The good news is that the messy period, for a lot of babies, is quite short; because the baby has the chance to practice feeding herself so often, she quickly gets good at it. There are lots of ways to prepare for the mess (see pages 100–03) and, as many parents quickly discover, spoon-feeding can be pretty messy, too!

> **"William didn't have any purées at all and it was quite a success. He's not a fussy eater like his brother, Samuel, who was spoon-fed. He loves the kind of things that most children won't touch; he likes black pepper and spicy food. People have said the range of food that William eats is quite amazing, compared to other children. He'll try anything."**
>
> Pete, father of Samuel, 5 years; William, 2 years; and Edward, 6 months

2 How Does Baby-Led Weaning Work?

"The beauty is that the readiness is so obvious. When a baby can sit up, reach out, pick food up and put it in his mouth, move it around and swallow it, his guts are ready. Nature would not have gotten it wrong."

Hazel, mother of Evie, 8 years;
Sam, 5 years; and Jacky, 22 months

Growing Skills

Learning to eat solid food is a natural part of a baby's development—just like crawling, walking, and talking. It's a normal part of growing up. Although some babies develop faster than others, the progress of all babies follows a set pattern, and new skills are acquired in more or less the same order for every baby. For example, most babies will learn how to do these skills in the following order.

- Roll over
- Sit up

- Crawl
- Stand up
- Walk

This principle works for all aspects of a baby's development, including feeding. Babies develop these skills without having to be taught them. In other words, they don't really "learn" them, they just become able to do them. Some skills develop gradually and others seem to appear overnight, but they are all the result of the baby practicing movements and putting them together. These skills are developing continuously, right from the moment the baby is born. Many early movements are instinctive, but, as babies gain more control over their muscles, they begin to be able to do things purposefully.

All babies develop skills that are related to feeding themselves, although babies who have the chance to practice—by handling food—are likely to become good at them earlier than babies who are spoon-fed. Babies naturally develop feeding-related skills in this order:

- Latch on to mother's breast
- Reach out toward interesting things
- Grab objects and take them to their mouth
- Explore things with lips and tongue
- Bite off a piece of food
- Chew
- Actively move food to the back of the mouth so it can be swallowed

- Pick up small objects using "pincer grip" (thumb and forefinger).

At birth, almost all babies can instinctively find their own way to the breast and latch on to feed. They also have a basic swallowing reflex. The suckling action used at the breast or on a bottle takes milk to the back of the baby's mouth, where the swallowing mechanism is triggered.

From about three months, babies start finding their hands: They catch sight of them, begin to wave them in front of their face, and study them. If anything touches their palm, their fist spontaneously closes around it. Gradually, they begin to bring their hands purposefully to their mouth. At this age their muscles are still not very well coordinated—babies may hit themselves in the face by mistake or seem surprised to find that they have something in their hand.

By about four months, a baby can reach out toward things that interest him. As his movements become more refined, he'll start to be able to move his arms and hands accurately to grab hold of interesting objects and bring them to his mouth. His lips and tongue are very sensitive, and the baby uses them to learn about the taste, texture, shape, and size of whatever he is holding.

All babies are curious about their surroundings, and, by the time they are six months old, most babies can grasp things and get them to their mouth fairly accurately. If a baby has the opportunity to look at, reach for, and grab food, he will bring it to his mouth, just as he would a toy. However, although it looks as though he is feeding himself, he won't actually swallow the food—he'll just explore it with his lips and tongue.

Atypical development

Reaching out for objects and mouthing them is part of regular infant development. While many six-month-old babies are not ready to start eating solid food, most are keen to begin exploring it with their hands and mouth. However, a very small number of babies have a physical condition (such as a muscle weakness in the arms or an abnormality of the mouth) that prevents them from developing these skills. In rare cases, such a condition may remain unnoticed until solid foods are introduced. If a baby of six months is not grasping objects, taking them to his mouth, and gnawing on them, it's probably a good idea for his general development to be reviewed by a pediatrician.

Between six and nine months, several abilities develop, one after the other. First, the baby manages to bite or gnaw off a small piece of food with his gums (or his teeth, if he has any). Soon after this, he discovers how to keep the food in his mouth for a short while. Because the size and shape of the inside of his mouth has changed as he's grown, he now has more control of his tongue so he is able to move the food around and chew it. At this stage though, as long as he is sitting upright, it will almost certainly fall out of his mouth rather than be swallowed.

Unlike milk (from a breast or bottle), which is sucked directly to the back of the baby's mouth, solid food needs to be actively moved there. This is something that a baby is unable to do until *after* he has discovered how to bite and chew. This means that, for a week or two at least, and provided he is sitting upright and is not distracted, any food he gets into his mouth will eventually fall back out again. He will only begin to swallow it when the muscles of his tongue, cheeks, and jaw are sufficiently coordinated to work together to enable him to gather the chewed food into a "bolus" and move it purposefully toward his throat. This may well be a natural safeguard to help minimize the chances of choking, but it only works as long as it's the baby who puts the food into his mouth—he needs to be in control.

At around nine months, the baby will develop the "pincer grip"—a way of using his thumb and forefinger to pick up small objects (or food). Before this happens, it's unlikely he will be able to get anything very small, such as a raisin or a pea, to his mouth.

Babies who are allowed to feed themselves at every mealtime get lots of chances to practice these skills and quickly become confident and adept. Just as babies will walk when they are ready, so, it seems, they will start to eat solid foods when they are ready—provided they are given the opportunity.

> **"As soon as someone explained BLW to me, I thought: *Of course—it makes sense!* I felt foolish for not having instinctively known it when I had my first baby. So with John, we knew he would feed himself; we had seen from the other two that it's perfectly possible. You don't have to do finger foods as an extra to spoon-feeding; it can be the only way of feeding."**
>
> Liz, mother of Heather, 8 years,
> Edwin, 5 years; and John, 20 months

BLW STORY

I'm not sure whether I would have done BLW instinctively if Arne hadn't shown me. When he was almost six months old, he was sitting next to my eldest child, Evie, one day as she watched TV, and he just grabbed her sandwich and took a bite out of it! But having something to eat was his choice, rather than me doing something to him; he got what he wanted when he wanted it. He was happy.

It was so different from feeding Evie. She was barely five months when we started solids, and it was horrible. I'm pretty sure I cried the first time I fed her; she couldn't sit up properly so she was in a recliner chair with purée just dribbling out of her mouth. And it was such a huge effort to express enough milk to make things runny enough.

So we'd already decided to wait a while with Arne anyway, and then after he'd taken the sandwich we tried mushing some food for him, but he didn't like being fed so we thought, "Why not just give him chunks of things?"

He would eat his broccoli first and then his carrot and then he would have meat or something—he was much more balanced and self-regulated than my daughter. With her, there were definitely phases where she'd refuse a whole load of food; all the effort of puréeing and she'd not want to eat. It felt very tortuous. The whole process was just so much easier with Arne, so we are doing the same with George.

Polly, mother of Evie, 6 years;
Arne, 4 years; and George, 6 months

Breast or bottle: Is there a difference for BLW?

There hasn't been any research into possible differences between how babies take to baby-led weaning, depending on whether they are breastfed or bottle-fed or have experienced a combination of the two. We do know that breast milk changes in flavor according to what the mother has eaten, so breastfed babies will expect the taste of family foods, and we know that breastfeeding involves a chewing-type action, which may also help to prepare babies for complementary foods. We also know that the end of milk feedings needs to be approached in a slightly different way for formula-fed babies (see page 219).

Anecdotally, however, there's nothing to suggest that there's any difference in the way babies approach BLW according to whether they've been breast- or bottle-fed. Some babies who are used to bottles and formula dig in to solid food right away while others take much longer—and it's the same for breastfed babies. A few parents who have bottle-fed find relying completely on their baby to take what he needs can be a challenge, especially in the beginning; for others, this seems to happen effortlessly once they see their baby with food. Yet others find that BLW offers their baby the opportunity to control his eating in a way that may have been lost.

So there's no reason to expect your baby to respond to baby-led weaning in any particular way according to whether he's breastfed, bottle-fed, or both. Provided you allow him the freedom he needs, he will do BLW *his* way!

Self-Feeding: A Natural Skill

Self-feeding is natural for babies. As soon as they find the breast and suckle, they are able to control how fast they feed and how much breast milk they take, according to how hungry or thirsty they are. Babies who are bottle-fed have these skills, too, but they are reliant on whoever is feeding them to be responsive to their cues, so their control over feeding is slightly less.

The ability to self-feed doesn't disappear; it develops and matures as the baby grows. Most parents wouldn't anticipate having to feed a child of two or three years old; they would expect him to feed himself. It doesn't seem logical that the natural progression of self-feeding should need to be interrupted by spoon-feeding, only for parents to have to decide when to allow the baby to go back to feeding himself.

There is no need to step in and do things for your baby for a few months—and no need to decide when to step out again. He can just continue to feed himself all the way through.

The Motivation to Try Solid Foods

The motivation for a six-month-old baby to take food to his mouth has nothing to do with hunger. Babies are curious about what's around them and instinctively want to copy what others are doing. So it's no surprise that they want to handle the food they see their parents picking up.

Most of our development as babies—maybe even all of it—is connected to survival. A baby needs to know which foods are safe and which are poisonous, so he watches his parents closely to see what they put in their mouths. This starts to happen at around the same time as he begins to work out how to use his arms and hands to grab things. A baby's curiosity is so intense that if he wants to grab an object, he will keep practicing the movements needed to get it, over and over again. And when he does manage to pick up something new, he almost always brings it to his mouth for exploring and testing. So when a baby first puts *food* in his mouth, he is treating it just as he would any other object. Until he gets it there, he has no idea that it has a particular taste or that it is edible. If he manages to bite a piece off, he will munch it with his gums, discovering what it feels and tastes like, but he is very unlikely to swallow it.

A baby who is allowed to take food to his mouth as soon as he can learns about the different textures and tastes of food long before he is able to swallow any. And he only very gradually discovers that food can stop him from feeling hungry. His motivation for handling food only changes once he has made the connection with hunger. This is usually any time from eight months to a year or so. This timing is perfect, since it's not until then that he really begins to need the food to provide him with nutrients.

Needing Extra Nutrients

There is a myth that breast milk changes at around six months and is no longer "enough" for a baby. In fact, the breast milk produced by the mother of a six-month-old baby (or even a two-year-old) has almost exactly the same nutritional value as it has always had; what changes is the baby's need for certain nutrients. Breast milk continues to be the most nutritionally balanced food for babies and children almost indefinitely.

Is it OK to start early?

The answer to this depends on what is meant by starting! Some babies begin to show an interest in food before they are six months old, sometimes even grabbing something from their parent's plate. This doesn't mean they're hungry or able to chew or digest solid food, so they may not be ready to actually eat any of the family dinner. But they are probably ready to start handling it.

When babies are spoon-fed, they are usually expected to eat the moment they are first presented with food, so the "start" of solid feeding is decided for them, whatever age they are. By contrast, the typical gap between a BLW baby's first encounter with food and his first swallowed mouthful means these two events happen days or even weeks apart, as determined by the baby.

With BLW, it's up to you when you start providing your baby with the opportunity to handle food, but it's up to him to decide when he's ready to pick it up and then when to start eating. Even if they are offered the opportunity earlier, very few BLW babies actually begin eating solid food before about six months.

BLW STORY

I really wanted to breastfeed, but when Charles had jaundice I was given the wrong information about what to do, and I ended up formula-feeding. But I still wanted him to have some control, so I was kind of feeding him on demand. To start with, the nurses said, "If he seems hungry, offer more formula." Then they said he was having too much and told me to space out his feedings. I think by four months he was having what a six-month-old should have. So when he started grumbling I didn't immediately put a bottle in his mouth. I played with him and distracted him. But he didn't have any control over his feeding. And it made me anxious, too. So I was looking for a way to give him back some control and to get back to the natural parenting that I had really wanted to do.

I found out about baby-led weaning online and it sounded really sensible, but at that time it seemed as though most of the advice was just for breastfed babies. But I realized there's no reason formula-fed babies shouldn't do it. By the time Charles was about three months, I'd decided that's what we would do. It was the best parenting decision I ever made. Charles took to it like a duck to water—he really went for it.

In a sense I think I found everything a bit easier because I was formula-feeding, so I could see exactly how much milk he was having. And on the days when he didn't really feel like eating, I could see his milk consumption go up, so I could see evidence that I could trust him. And starting solids this way did what I wanted it to do—it gave him some control back.

Rosie, mother of Charles, 9 years;
and Rowan, 6 years

Babies are born with stores of key nutrients, such as iron and zinc, accumulated during their time in the womb. These stores start to be used from the moment the baby is born, but the amounts in his milk feedings are enough to ensure that he still has plenty. From six months on, the balance shifts so that the baby begins very gradually to need more from his diet than breast milk or formula alone can supply.

It's important to recognize that, at six months, most babies are only just beginning to outgrow their milk-only diet. Most full-term babies have adequate stores of, for example, iron, to see them through for quite a bit longer without a problem—they don't run out of anything overnight. But they need to be introduced to solids at around six months so that they can develop the skills they need to eat different foods and get used to new tastes, ready for when they really do begin to rely on other foods as their main source of nourishment a few months later.

A baby's increasing need for more nutrients seems to coincide with the gradual development of his self-feeding skills. So at six months, when babies still have a good store of nutrients, almost all are beginning to pick up food and take it to their mouths. By around nine months, when the need for more nutrients is growing, most BLW babies have developed the skills they need to eat a wide range of family foods, which will provide them with the extra nourishment they need. It's at about this age (though it varies quite a bit from baby to baby) that many BLW parents report that their baby seems to be eating more purposefully—as though he instinctively knows that he actually needs this food in addition to his breast milk or formula feedings.

How cord clamping at birth affects a baby's nutrient stores

Since the 1960s, in most parts of the world, it has been routine to clamp and cut the umbilical cord immediately after a baby is born. However, research has shown that early cord clamping may affect a baby's health adversely.[1] If left unclamped, the umbilical cord continues to pulsate for up to five minutes, delivering nutrient-rich blood to the baby from the placenta. Cutting the cord before it has finished pulsating means the baby starts life outside the womb with less than the optimum supply of some key nutrients—especially iron. Leaving the cord to finish pulsating before it is clamped gives the baby plenty of iron to draw on for at least the first six months, and possibly longer.

The Importance of Milk Feedings

Between six and nine months, the amount of breast milk or formula your baby drinks should stay more or less the same while solid foods gradually increase. Parents sometimes feel under pressure to reduce their child's milk feedings so that he relies more on solid foods, but this isn't a good idea. It's only from about nine months that most babies begin to reduce their milk feedings and allow solid meals to start to take over.

If a baby is allowed to determine the start of solid feeding and the pace of its progress, he will follow his own natural path toward more solids and less milk.

Babies vary in the speed with which they come to grips with solid feeding and begin to move away from milk. Some babies start swallowing food almost right away, at around six months, and by nine months are competent self-feeders who are already beginning to cut down their milk feedings. Other babies start very gradually, showing no real interest in doing more than exploring solid foods until they are well over eight months, and still eating only small amounts at ten or even twelve months. And, of course, there are many variations in between. There are babies who start off very enthusiastically but who seem to slow down after a few weeks. And there are others who seem to take ages to take any interest in solids but, once they do, progress with amazing speed.

Many babies do things in bursts, alternating weeks when nothing much seems to happen with weeks when they're doing something new every day. All of this is completely normal and is very different from the sort of steady, stage-by-stage progress that parents are led to expect when their baby is on puréed foods.

> **"One of the problems I have with conventional weaning is the 'stages' babies are supposed to go through; BLW blows all that out of the water."**
>
> Helen, dietitian

Babies don't need teeth to chew

Babies of six months quite often have one or more teeth, but not all do. Whether or not their teeth have started to come in doesn't seem to make much difference to their ability to bite, gnaw, or chew most foods, although very hard foods, such as raw carrot, will have to wait. Gums are very good for biting and munching—as any breastfeeding mother who has had a nip from a teething baby will tell you!

> **"Otis hasn't got any teeth yet. The other two didn't get any teeth at all until they were over a year old, so I know babies don't need teeth to chew—at a year they were both eating normal family foods."**
>
> Sadie, mother of Ellen, 9 years; Thomas, 5 years; and Otis, 8 months

Developing the Ability to Chew

Many people assume that babies need to be taught to chew by starting them off on smooth purées and progressing gradually to lumpier food. This isn't the case. Babies naturally become able to manage chewable foods as their mouths grow and develop. They make progress by practicing on foods that stimulate chewing, not on foods that can be swallowed without needing to be chewed at all.

In the past, learning to take food off a spoon was seen as a key developmental skill, but we now know that it was connected to a reflex that babies outgrow naturally. For the first few months, babies display an extrusion reflex, or "tongue thrust," which they use (unconsciously) to push anything but the breast or bottle out of their mouth. This is probably a safety mechanism, to prevent anything solid from being swallowed or inhaled. Trying to spoon-feed a very young baby involves overriding this reflex, which is why it's so difficult and messy. The tongue-thrust reflex naturally begins to fade at about four months of age, whether or not the baby has been spoon-fed. So what used to be described as a baby "getting used to the spoon" was, in fact, just the tongue-thrust reflex disappearing.

As adults, we tend to take for granted the way we use the muscles of our mouth. But the way you move chewing gum from one cheek to the other, how you separate a cherry or an olive from its pit to spit the pit out, or what you do to retrieve a fish bone or a piece of food that is stuck in your teeth are quite complex movements. Learning to use your tongue to move food around your mouth is important for safety and good oral hygiene as well as for eating and speaking—and the best way to learn these skills is to practice them on lots of foods with different textures.

Crunchy, chewy, sticky, and runny foods all produce different sensations in the mouth and need to be managed in a different way. The more a baby is allowed to experience different textures, the more likely he is to become skilled at dealing with them and the more willing he'll be to try new foods.

Is There Really a Window of Opportunity?

Some people refer to the period between four and six months as a "window of opportunity" for getting babies used to new tastes and textures. They worry that, if this period is missed, the baby will be reluctant to accept solid foods and introducing them will be difficult as a result. This concern seems to stem from the fact that babies who don't have their first spoonful of solid food until after they reach six months appear to be more resistant to the idea than younger babies.

Unfortunately, because spoon-feeding has been the accepted way to feed babies for so long, researchers are only just beginning to question whether it might be the *feeding* that these babies are refusing, rather than the *food*. Babies of six months and older who are allowed to self-feed are, in fact, very keen to try new foods; they are also capable little people who like to do things for themselves. So if there *is* an ideal period for babies to get used to new tastes and textures, it probably doesn't start until they naturally begin to take food to their mouths, at around six months.

Eating Enough but Not Too Much: Understanding Appetite Control

Knowing when to stop eating is a key factor in avoiding obesity and maintaining the right weight for your size, however old you are, so stopping when you've had enough sounds like common sense. But many children—and adults—are unable to do this.

Many parents worry that their baby or child isn't eating enough. Food is intrinsically linked with nurturing and love: We all want to show our babies how much we love them, and giving them food is one way to do this. At the same time, we can feel a sense of rejection when our child turns down the food we have prepared for him. These emotions, combined with unrealistic expectations of how much food babies should eat (see page 159), mean that many babies and older children are regularly persuaded to eat more than they need. This can mean that the child simply learns to overeat. In extreme cases, it can lead to problems such as food refusal or phobias; either way, the development of normal appetite control is at risk.

Persuading young babies to eat food they don't want is especially easy to do if they are spoon-fed. Babies who are allowed to feed themselves, on the other hand, will naturally manage their own intake—they simply stop eating when they've had enough. This means they eat as much as they need—and no more.

> **"Erin has a great attitude toward food. She can control her own appetite—she simply eats when she's hungry and stops when she's full. Our eating is so messed up in this country it's really hard for some people to understand how good that is."**
>
> Judith, mother of Erin, 2 years

How fast we eat is important, too, not least because eating too fast has also been linked with obesity. Many parents choose to spoon-feed babies and young children simply because it's quicker than allowing them to feed themselves. If a baby is allowed to feed himself, he will eat at his own pace, taking as much time as he needs to deal with a particular piece of food. Parents are often surprised at how long their baby can spend chewing one mouthful. Being in control of how much and how quickly he eats not only makes the meal more enjoyable for him but means that the baby is able to more easily recognize when he's had enough.

Many of the eating problems that affect older children and their families appear to have their roots in issues of who has control. Indeed, health professionals who work with these families commonly start by asking the parents to "give control back to the child." Maybe if this control isn't taken away in the first place, problems like food refusal and overeating won't be as common.

> **"I found with spoon-feeding it was harder to know whether or not Tristan had actually finished when he didn't want anymore or whether it was part of the power game as to who was going to have the spoon."**
>
> Andrew, father of Tristan, 4 years; and Madeleine, 7 months

> **"I like the fact that, with BLW, the baby is in control. I see lots of babies who are dysfunctional feeders, and it's nearly always because they have no control."**
>
> Helen, dietitian

Won't He Choke?

Research has shown that BLW carries no greater risk of choking than spoon-feeding.[2] But the possibility of choking is still a worry for many parents and grandparents who aren't used to seeing babies feed themselves. Provided you take basic safety precautions (see pages 81–82), BLW may even make choking less likely.

Sitting upright

Your baby needs to be able to sit upright—without slumping or leaning back—before he starts handling solid food, to allow him to reach it comfortably and help prevent him from choking. However, this doesn't mean he has to be able to get himself into a sitting position unaided or sit for any length of time without any support. Indeed most babies can't do this until they are around eight months old. The most important thing is that he should be able to hold his head and trunk erect, even though he may need a little support around his hips to enable him to reach forward easily (see Chapter 3).

Often, worries about choking are based on seeing babies gagging on food, or coughing and spluttering while eating, and assuming they are choking. In fact, the gagging and coughing reflexes act to *protect* a baby from choking.

The gag reflex

Gagging is a retching movement that pushes food forward if the amount is too big to be swallowed. It's part of the same movement as vomiting. Gagging doesn't seem to bother babies who are feeding themselves, and they usually carry on eating as if nothing has happened.

In an adult, the gag response is triggered near the back of the tongue—you have to put your finger right back toward your throat to make it happen. If you do this, you will feel the back part of your tongue rise up, pushing forward anything that is there while at the same time closing off your airway and preventing the food from entering it. However, it seems that this reflex is triggered farther forward on the tongue of a six-month-old baby, so not only is it activated more easily than it is in an adult, it also operates when the piece of food that has caused it is farther away from the airway. So, when babies of six or seven months gag on food, it very rarely means they are in danger of choking.

The gag reflex may well be a key part of babies' learning how to manage food safely. When a baby has triggered this reflex a few times by putting too much food into his mouth or pushing it too far back, he learns not to do it. As he gets older, the reflex lessens, whether or not he has been allowed to experiment with self-feeding, meaning that gagging doesn't happen until food is nearer to the back of his mouth. However, this also means that it becomes less effective as an early warning sign. So babies who haven't been allowed to explore food from the beginning may miss the opportunity to use this reflex to help them learn how to eat safely. There is evidence that babies who have been spoon-fed have more problems with gagging when they start to handle food (often at around eight months) than those who have been allowed to experiment much earlier.

While gagging is not a cause for concern, it's important to

remember that this response is essentially a safety mechanism. For it to work effectively, the baby must be sitting upright, so that any food that has gone too far back in his mouth is pushed forward—not backward—by the reflex.

Gagging, coughing, and spoon-feeding

Many instances of babies gagging or coughing are actually related to spoon-feeding, especially when lumpy foods are given by spoon. To understand why this is, think about how you use a spoon to eat a smooth soup and compare it with the way you eat breakfast cereal. If you were to slurp your cereal the way you do your soup, the lumps would go straight to the back of your throat and you would soon start to cough and splutter. When babies are spoon-fed, they tend to suck the food in, so they gag or cough very easily.

For a baby, puréed food can be especially difficult to deal with because it's harder to push forward than more-solid food that has been partially chewed, making gagging more prolonged and stressful.

The cough reflex

Coughing happens when the airway is under threat. During coughing, the airway is open and whatever is threatening to block it is propelled forward, not by the tongue (as in gagging) but by a sharp blast of air from the lungs. Coughing can be triggered by something as small as a crumb or a teaspoonful of liquid. It's common for an adult to have a fit of coughing if they're distracted or start to laugh while eating something crumbly, such as a cookie.

When something partially blocks or irritates a baby's airway, he automatically starts to cough to clear it. Most babies have a very efficient cough reflex and, provided they are upright or leaning forward, it is usually best not to disturb them while this reflex is in operation. The coughing and spluttering that look and sound so alarming are actually signs that your baby is dealing with the problem.

> **"To start with, when Izaak coughed when he was eating, we would jump up, get him out of the chair, and hit him on the back. But when we stopped and actually looked at what he was doing, we realized that if we just allowed him the time to cough something back up, it would always come out and he would just carry on eating quite happily."**
>
> Lucy, mother of Izaak, 8 months

Choking

True choking is very rare. It occurs when the gag and cough reflexes have been bypassed and no air can get past the obstruction. A baby who is truly choking is usually silent; he is unable to cough and needs someone else to dislodge the lump for him using first aid measures. Four factors make choking more likely:

- Offering food that is thought to be a particular choking risk (see pages 119–20)
- Someone else putting food (or drink) into the baby's mouth

- A leaning-back position
- The baby being distracted while eating (for example, by games, the TV, or being hurried).

Imagine someone approaching you with some food on a spoon, ready to feed you. Chances are you would reach out to stop them so that you could check what the food was and how much was on the spoon. You would want to control when and how it went into your mouth. These basic checks would let you predict how to deal with the food once it was inside your mouth. Planning how to deal with food helps to prevent choking.

If you were leaning back, the situation would be even more frightening because gravity would be more likely to take the food to the back of your mouth before you were ready to swallow it. When we relate this to adults, it's clear that the person who is eating needs to be in control of the feeding process. The same thing applies to babies.

When a baby puts a piece of food into his mouth himself, he is in control of it. If he is able to chew it, he will. If he is able to get it to the back of his throat, he'll swallow it. If he isn't able to do these things, then, as long as he is upright, the food will simply fall out. Allowing a baby to feed himself means that he is in control—and having control helps to keep him safe.

The opportunity to handle food is another important part of mealtime safety. As adults, we can anticipate how most foods will feel and behave inside our mouths by their color, shape, and texture, based on our experience. Babies don't have any experience to draw on; they are building a completely new set of connections. Exploring food with their hands enables them to start to make predictions about how best to manage each mouthful—and to judge which pieces may be too big, chewy, or hard for them to tackle.

The link between his developing manual dexterity and what he can do with his mouth may also help to keep a BLW baby safe. When a six-month-old baby first starts to feed himself, he can't pick up the sorts of food that he might have trouble moving around with his tongue, such as raisins and peas, so they are unlikely to get into his mouth. It's only as he gets to about nine months that he will begin to use his finger and thumb in the pincer grip that enables him to grasp tiny objects. By this time, provided he has been allowed to practice feeding himself with foods of different textures, his chewing skills will be well advanced. This means that once he *can* get a raisin to his mouth he will almost certainly be able to manage it safely. This coming together of two key aspects of babies' development is a fundamental part of what makes BLW a safe approach.

> **"Magnus (who was spoon-fed) sometimes puts too much food in his mouth and then gags—and sometimes almost chokes. This happens often with meat (my husband had to pull some squid out of his mouth once, and I've had to whack him on the back hard once or twice). Leon (who was BLW'd) gagged a few times, but he has never choked."**
>
> Joy, mother of Magnus, 6 years; and Leon, 3 years

Do Babies Really Know What They Need to Eat?

When babies are allowed to choose what they want to eat from the foods offered at mealtimes, their parents are often surprised by how well balanced the baby's chosen diet is over the course of a week or so. There has been little reliable research into whether babies really do know instinctively what to eat, but the self-selection experiment in the 1920s by an American pediatrician, Dr. Clara Davis,[3] is certainly food for thought (see below). At the time, the recommended diet for most babies was strictly limited, and Dr. Davis's lesson about the importance of giving them a range of foods proved very influential. However, her idea that they might be allowed to choose what to eat seems to have been lost—probably because in later years babies began to be given solids at three or four months, when they aren't yet capable of making these choices.

Dr. Clara Davis's self-selection experiment

In the 1920s, Dr. Davis had a theory that babies and young children know best when it comes to what they need to eat, so she decided to see what would happen if they were allowed to choose for themselves. All the children were aged between seven and nine months when the experiment started and had been exclusively breastfed up until that point (as was common at the time). They were offered thirty-three foods, with a slightly different selection at each meal. All the foods were nutritious and unprocessed. They were presented separately, mashed and unseasoned, and the babies could choose whatever they wanted to eat, in any combination and in any quantity. They either fed themselves or pointed to a dish and were spoon-fed by a nurse.

Dr. Davis found that each child chose a very well-balanced diet. Even though their food combinations were unique and unpredictable by adult standards, all the children were well nourished and healthy at the end of the experiment—including those who hadn't been at the start. They ate a greater variety and quantity of food than was considered normal for their age. Food fads or bingeing were common (one toddler apparently ate seven eggs in one day!), but they were balanced by other choices on other days. All the children were willing to try unfamiliar foods—and none of them chose the baby cereal and milk-based diet that babies were "supposed" to eat at the time.

BLW STORY

Our second child, Saskia, would sit on my lap while we ate, and she started reaching for food from our plates when she was just under six months old. She was happy grabbing food and putting it in her mouth, so we sort of intuitively did BLW without really thinking about it. And later I realized there were other people who were doing it and it had a name. It's so easy; mothers must have been doing it, especially with second babies, for generations.

In retrospect, I think our first child, Lily, was reaching for food, but we just did what is accepted wisdom for feeding babies—we spoon-fed her. We'd take turns; one of us would eat, and the other would feed Lily.

Baby-led weaning is quicker and easier—and messier. It *is* messy. But spoon-feeding is complicated. It's another little thing to be slightly anxious about. And it's boring. We were always either preparing food, or feeding or cleaning up. It was so food-oriented, the purée thing. This seems to be much more just enjoying mealtimes and playing. It's much more relaxed.

Suzanne, mother of Lily, 3 years; and Saskia, 14 months

Baby-Led Weaning and Babies Born Preterm

Babies who are born early may have specific needs when it comes to introducing solid foods, but it really depends on how many weeks premature the baby is. While a pregnancy of thirty-six or thirty-seven weeks can be considered almost full-term, one of only twenty-seven weeks obviously cannot. Also, many premature babies are not just born early but are also extremely small, or even ill, or there may be reasons why they were born early that have a bearing on their later development. Clearly, one recommendation won't do for them all.

Baby-led weaning works for a baby born at term because his nutritional need for solid food and his developmental readiness—or ability—to feed himself coincide, so he can feed himself with solids as soon as he needs to (usually sometime after six months). A premature baby's general development continues at more or less the same pace as if he had been born when he was due—so if he arrived six weeks early, he probably won't show an interest in food or be able to get it to his mouth until he is around seven and a half months. But it's quite possible that he will need some additional nutrients before this because he hasn't had enough time in the womb to build up the normal reserves.

Not a great deal is known about the needs of preterm babies when it comes to solid food, and there's no consensus about how babies should be given extra nutrients if they do need them before they can feed themselves. Some babies are prescribed supplements in the form of medicine; others may be given puréed food, in which case a short period of spoon-feeding will be necessary. Each baby needs to be treated as an individual. However, there is no reason why preterm babies who don't need additional nutrients, or who are having them as medicine, shouldn't be allowed to take their time with solids, even if this means they don't show an interest until they are well past six months.

In general, all babies of six months or more should be encouraged to explore food with their hands and be given the opportunity to feed themselves as soon as they appear interested. However, if your baby was born prematurely or has particular medical or physical problems, you should seek advice from his pediatrician, dietitian, or speech and language therapist before deciding whether to use BLW as the only method for introducing him to solid foods.

> **"Sean was born four weeks early and, when I started BLW, it all felt quite new to me, having spoon-fed Lorna. I think he was a little 'behind' his peers, as they were all term babies, but doing BLW gave him the chance to show us when he was ready."**
>
> Rachel, mother of Lorna, 14 years; and Sean, 4 years

Baby-Led Weaning in Special Cases

The concept of baby-led weaning revolves around typical infant development, but this doesn't mean that babies whose health or development is compromised should be denied the opportunity for autonomy at mealtimes.

Babies who have delayed development, muscle weakness, or physical abnormalities of the mouth, hands, arms, or back (such as Down syndrome or cerebral palsy) may not be able to meet all their nutritional needs without help, but shared mealtimes and self-feeding shouldn't be ruled out. In fact, BLW can sometimes be an ideal way to help these babies develop precisely the skills that they find difficult. For example, the repeated hand-to-mouth movements involved in self-feeding can help develop fine motor skills and hand-eye coordination. Babies whose core muscles are weak get a mini-workout every time they lean forward to pick up a piece of food, while biting and chewing helps those who lack strength or mobility in their jaws and tongue.

> **"I've used BLW with many babies with Down syndrome and the results are amazing! It's all about what they can do, not what they can't."**
>
> Jill, speech pathologist, feeding therapist, and lactation consultant

It may take a little longer for babies who face extra challenges to begin to feed themselves efficiently, and some may need a transitional phase or professional support. However, even a modified version of BLW can make all the difference in enabling a baby to eat with his family and develop self-confidence.

Babies with digestive problems

Puréed solid foods are sometimes recommended for babies with gastroesophageal reflux disease (GERD), but there is no real evidence that this is either necessary or makes any difference. It seems just as likely that any improvement in the condition is related to the baby's ability to sit upright, rather than to the food he is given.

Babies with serious or complex digestive disorders may need special foods that can't be made into suitable shapes for self-feeding, but this shouldn't prevent them from handling at least some of their food themselves.

BLW STORY

I was pregnant when we found out that our second child, Zephaniah, had Down syndrome. It was a huge shock, and we had no idea what to expect. I wondered what would happen with breastfeeding and solids. I did BLW with my daughter, and I'd been really excited about doing it again.

After he was born, I began to think more and more about doing baby-led weaning, especially as six months approached. I'm passionate about wanting Zephaniah to be as independent with as many skills as possible. But babies with Down syndrome can have low muscle tone—they often sit up later than their peers—and I worried whether he would be able to coordinate chewing and swallowing.

As a mother of a baby with additional needs, the important word for me so far is *inclusion*. What better way to promote a sense of inclusion than at the dinner table?

When Zephaniah turned six months old, he was very close to sitting without support, but he wasn't quite ready. At seven months, he tried a slice of avocado, but he struggled initially to pick it up, so I put it in his hand. He knew what to do with it. The next thing I gave him was a sweet potato wedge. After this, I quickly moved to giving him whatever we were having.

I've never spoon-fed him. He's always fed himself. The only adaptation I made was during the very first few weeks when I would hand him the food. And I'd hand him preloaded spoons of yogurt or soup. He really didn't eat a lot until probably nine to ten months, but he always loved exploring and trying everything. Since he turned twelve months, I've noticed a reduction in breastfeeding.

It has been an amazing experience, and he has such a great relationship with food and eating. It's wonderful that we can all sit down together and eat. I know we have helped him develop skills that will assist him throughout his life. His fine motor abilities have really come along, which helps in other therapies we do, and I'm convinced that BLW has contributed to that hugely. All the health professionals we see are super-impressed with him!

Sarah, mother of Zephaniah, 15 months

3 Getting Started

"Lara sat at the table with us while we ate for a few weeks before she had her first taste of food. She would follow the food to our mouths with her eyes and 'air chew' along with us. Then one day she took some bread from my hand, stared at it for a while, and slowly brought it to her mouth. She missed and poked herself in the cheek. I had to fight the urge to help her, and eventually she found her mouth. She sucked and chomped on the bread—I don't think she actually swallowed anything. But the excitement and pride I felt was quite ridiculous."

Emma, mother of Lara, 7 months

Preparing for BLW

Once your baby is nearly six months old, you may find that she wants to join in with family mealtimes, even though she is not quite able to sit up and reach for food. Babies are intensely curious at this age and are happiest when they feel included. Letting your baby sit with you will make her feel part of what's going on. When she's ready to start handling food, she'll let you know.

You don't have to buy any special equipment for BLW, and although there are some products that may make your life a little easier, they aren't essential. A high chair may be useful, but many parents start offering solids simply by sitting their baby on their lap during mealtimes and letting her play with food from their plate. Whatever you decide, once your baby begins exploring food, make sure she can't fall and that she is supported in a fully upright position.

Healthy family foods can be adapted easily so that your baby can manage them, so there's no need to buy or prepare any special foods for her (see Chapter 4 for more on what to offer and the few foods you need to avoid). And there's no need for any cutlery for the first few months, as your baby will use her fingers; just make sure her hands are clean before she starts.

Finally, you may want to prepare for some mess—a baby learning about food can be very messy in the early months (see pages 100–03 for tips).

> **"James always sat on my lap at mealtimes, and he started grabbing food and getting it to his mouth at about seven months. One of the first things he had was a really tender piece of steak! I made a stew and I offered him a big chunk of meat and he just sucked on it and maybe gummed some of the fibers. He looked as if he was really enjoying it."**
>
> Sarah, mother of James, 2 years

When to Eat

Although many books on introducing solids suggest timetables for feeding babies in the first few weeks or months, this isn't necessary. In the past, when parents were advised to offer food once a day, then progress in stages to two and three meals over a period of a few weeks, the guidance was aimed at babies who were starting solids at three or four months of age, when their digestive system was really too immature. Babies of six months and over are less likely to react badly to new foods because their gut is more mature. All you need to do at six months is to start to include your baby whenever you eat—it could be at breakfast, lunch, dinner, or when you have a snack—as long as she isn't tired or grumpy.

It's especially important that your baby isn't hungry when you sit her down to explore food, because in the early weeks of solids, mealtimes have nothing to do with hunger. They are about play, sharing, and copying others—opportunities to learn rather than to actually eat. (This is very different from the conventional way of introducing solids, when you are generally advised to make sure your baby is hungry at mealtimes.) If your baby *is* hungry when you share a meal, she won't be able to enjoy exploring food and developing her self-feeding skills—she'll simply get frustrated and upset, just as she would if she were handed a new toy when what she really wanted was milk.

> "I can't believe how close I came to giving up BLW in the beginning. Stephanie just didn't seem interested in solids at all—I thought it wasn't working. But one day she was really fractious before lunch, so I gave her a quick breastfeed. I sat her in the high chair and couldn't believe it when she picked up some carrot and started to chew on it! It was only then that I finally realized what I was doing wrong—I just needed to give her the solids when she wasn't hungry."
>
> Annabel, mother of Zoe, 2 years; and Stephanie, 8 months

Baby-led weaning works best if you are giving your baby her milk feedings whenever she wants them. That way she can take as much milk as she needs and enjoy exploring solid foods as a separate activity. Remember, she has no idea yet that solid food can fill her tummy, so if you think she is getting hungry when you have a meal planned, offer her a milk feeding. If she's too sleepy after her feed to be interested in solids, don't worry—you can simply offer her something later, when she is more alert.

It doesn't matter if you miss meals at this stage, since your baby won't be relying on them for nourishment for another few months. Although it's good to give her as many opportunities to practice her feeding skills as you can, there's no need to insist that she join in every meal or to feel that you have to keep her awake for an evening meal (see page 98). Eventually, most parents end up adapting mealtimes to fit in with when their child is hungry, but this probably won't be necessary until she's around a year old.

The interest your baby takes in food will probably be unpredictable from day to day. She may want to eat at every meal for three days and then go back to milk feedings only for the next four days. This natural progression of two steps forward, one step back is nothing like the strict timetables that parents are sometimes encouraged to follow. Provided you let your baby stay in control of the process, she will build up her intake of solid food gradually. That way she can continue to take all the breast milk or formula she needs, adjusting at a pace that is right for her without filling up on foods that are less nutritious.

Basic Safety

Some of these basic safety rules apply to spoon-feeding, too, but others are particularly important for a baby who is feeding herself. Sharing this information with anyone who is looking after your baby will help to keep her mealtimes safe, whomever she is with:

- Your baby should be sitting upright to handle food (see page 62). If necessary, use your hands to keep her stable on your lap or, if she's in a high chair, tuck a small rolled-up towel around her hips. Leaning back while eating can be dangerous, so never offer her food in a reclining chair, stroller, or car seat.
- Don't offer your baby foods that are a choking hazard. Some foods should be avoided completely (such as whole nuts); other potentially risky foods can be adapted to make them safer to handle (see page 135).

- Don't let anyone but your baby put food into her mouth. If she can't get it there herself, she's probably not ready to manage it safely. Watch out for toddlers or others trying to "help"!
- Let your baby concentrate while she's handling food. Don't hurry her or distract her—she needs to take her time to eat safely.
- Never leave your baby alone with food.

Finger Food

The key to BLW in the early months is to offer food that is easy and safe for your baby to pick up and bring to her mouth. Although you can let her have almost anything she can grab from your plate (see pages 119–23 for the exceptions), it will be less frustrating for her if you include foods of a shape and size that she can manage easily.

Babies of six months use their whole hand to pick things up in a palmar grip; they can't usually grasp small things with their thumb and forefinger until they're a few months older. This means they must be able to close their hand around a piece of food to hold it, so it mustn't be so wide or thick that they can't do this.

Babies of this age also need the food to stick out beyond their palm because they can't open their fist on purpose to get to it. When your baby is first starting, her aim won't be very accurate, so long pieces of food stand a better chance of being picked up than short ones. Sticks or "fingers" of food, at least two inches (five centimeters) long, mean that half the length is available for eating while the other half is the handle to hold it with. There's no need to be exact—you'll soon see what your baby can manage. Broccoli is an ideal first food because it already has a handle—but all kinds of fruit and vegetables, and most meat, can be cut into a rough finger shape.

If you are offering vegetables, bear in mind they shouldn't be too soft (or they'll turn to mush when your baby tries to handle them) or too hard (or she won't be able to gnaw them easily). See Chapter 4 for more information on how to adapt your food for your baby.

A baby of six or seven months will normally gnaw or munch on the part of the food that sticks out of her fist. She may bite off a small piece and will then probably drop the rest as she goes to pick up something else. This isn't a sign that she doesn't like the food, just that she is not yet able to open her hand on purpose or to concentrate on two things at once. By about eight months your baby will be able to get at food inside her fist and, as her skills develop, you will find she can manage smaller pieces and more awkward shapes and no longer needs the handle.

> "I cut everything into finger shapes at the beginning, but I didn't realize that they weren't quite long enough. Lucy couldn't move her hand down or release the food. There was nothing poking out of her fist to eat. She must have been so frustrated. I just didn't know what she could and couldn't do. I found out some time later that food needed to be long enough to have a handle for her to hold."
>
> Laura, mother of Josie, 10 years; and Lucy, 17 months

Improving Coordination

Once babies can pick up pieces of food accurately and are learning to open their fist to get at food inside it, they often go through a phase of using two hands to feed themselves. This is all part of developing coordination. At this stage they can find it easier to reach their mouth if they use their other hand to guide the hand with the food in it. Once your baby figures this out, you will probably notice that she misses her mouth much less frequently.

In the early stages, some babies also use one or both hands to keep the food in their mouth while they chew it. This is because they haven't yet discovered how to open and close their jaws without opening and closing their lips. As soon as your baby has learned to keep her lips closed while chewing, she will be able to use her hands to get the next mouthful ready without the first one falling out!

Ouch!

Sometimes babies put their fingers into their mouth along with the food. This is fine, until they accidentally bite down a bit too hard on a finger (or bite their tongue by mistake)! If your baby suddenly cries while eating, this is probably what's happened. Unfortunately, there's nothing you can do to prevent it from happening—it's just something she has to find out for herself. So, until she figures it out, just be ready to give her a quick cuddle to comfort her.

By about nine months, your baby will be able to pick up small pieces between her finger and thumb (pincer grip), so she will be able to manage food such as soft raisins and peas. She will also be able to "dip" fairly accurately, so you can offer her soft foods such as hummus or yogurt to eat with a breadstick or a piece of rice cake, or she can dip with her fingers. (See pages 136–37 for more on runny foods.)

As long as you offer your baby plenty of food that she can pick up, it's good to let her experiment with foods that she is still too young to manage (see grid below). Handling lots of different textures and shapes will help her develop the skills she needs to eat a varied diet—and she may surprise you with what she can do.

> **"Millie has become better at manipulating food now; she'll turn broccoli around so she can eat the floret, because she knows she can eat that bit more easily. She's also worked out how to eat fruit or vegetables and leave the skin."**
>
> Beth, mother of Millie, 10 months

> **"Bronwyn's getting good now at scooping stuff into her mouth, rather than just holding on to a stick of something. And she picks up little bits, too, and puts her whole hand in her mouth and drops the food there. Then she has a good suck on her fingers, and then her hand comes out for more."**
>
> Faye, mother of William, 4 years; and Bronwyn, 7 months

Developing skills: what to expect

The grid below shows you roughly what you can expect to see your baby doing at different ages and the types of foods that will suit her abilities. As her skills develop, it's a good idea to offer her foods that she can manage fairly easily, so she doesn't get frustrated, alongside new textures and shapes, so that she can try them, too. Of course, each baby develops at a different pace, and there's no need to actively encourage your baby to learn any new skills. All she needs is plenty of opportunities to practice, and she'll get there in her own time.

AGE	WHAT YOUR BABY IS LIKELY TO DO	WHAT TO OFFER
From around 6 to 8 months	She'll start to reach and grasp food using her whole hand in what's known as a palmar grip. She won't be able to open her fist to get at what's inside it but will gum or gnaw at anything poking out of the top. She'll get to food to her mouth with increasing accuracy.	Large finger-shaped pieces of food (around 2 inches [5 cm] long and ½ to ¾ inches [1 to 2 cm] wide), such as strips of tender meat, vegetables and fruit, omelet, and meat or lentil patties. **Plus, to try:** soft food in clumps (such as ground beef, sticky rice, and oatmeal) and foods that are slippery (such as pasta with sauce); soft foods such as strawberries.
From around 7 to 9 months	She'll be able to open and close her fist and bite and hold on to slippery or soft foods more easily. She may use one hand to guide the other to get food to her mouth, and she may push or squeeze soft food into her mouth. Biting and chewing are likely to be more effective.	Finger-shaped foods and strips of meat, soft food in clumps, slippery foods and smaller soft foods. **Plus, to try:** a dipper with runny food (see pages 136–37); crunchier foods such as raw peppers.

AGE	WHAT YOUR BABY IS LIKELY TO DO	WHAT TO OFFER
From around 8 to 10 months	She'll start using her fingers to pick food up, rather than her whole hand. Coordinating both hands together will be easier, and she'll become more skilled at using a dipper.	All the food types already listed, plus smaller things such as rice, peas and raisins. **Plus, to try:** She may want to test out cutlery, so she may enjoy trying to spear small chunks of food with a fork and dipping a spoon into runny food (see pages 136–37).
From around 9 to 12 months	She'll begin to use a refined pincer grip to pick up very small pieces of food (such as grains of rice and crumbs) between her thumb and forefinger. Most babies start to eat more purposefully at this age and to experiment less with food.	A range of healthy foods in a variety of shapes and textures.
From around 11 to 14 months	She may be keen to practice with forks and spoons but will probably go back to using her fingers now and then for quite a while.	Any healthy food, remembering to include a variety of shapes, textures, and tastes.

Offering Rather Than Giving

We often talk about "giving" babies food, but all you're really doing with BLW is "offering" by placing suitable pieces within your baby's reach, on either your plate, the table, or her high chair tray, and then letting her decide what to do with it. She may play with it, drop it, smear it, take it to her mouth, or simply sniff it; but it's up to her whether or not she eats it.

It may be tempting to put things into your baby's mouth for her, however, not only is it more enjoyable for her to be in control, but it's also much safer; putting things into a baby's mouth can be a choking hazard (see page 65). It's also important to let her decide whether or not to pick something up, so she can choose what she is going to explore or eat; try to avoid making these decisions for her by putting pieces of food into her hand. It's OK to offer her something to take from your hand occasionally, but the more you can trust your baby to manage it in her own way and in her own time, the faster she'll learn and the more confident she'll become.

Remember to make sure that food isn't too hot before you offer it; taking a bite is a more reliable way to check than touching it with your lips or using your finger. A good tip is to put any hot food on a plate that has been in the fridge for half an hour, to help it cool down faster. Your baby is likely to feel left out if she has to wait for her meal to cool down while everyone else is digging in to theirs!

Microwave hot spots

If you microwave food, be sure to turn or stir it while it's cooking—microwaving can heat food unevenly, producing unexpected hot spots. Test the temperature before you offer any to your baby; a sample mouthful is the most effective way.

How Much Food to Offer

When your baby first starts handling solid foods, she'll be eating very little and playing a lot. For the first few weeks, pretty much all the food you give her will end up in the high chair or on the floor. In the early days, she may lose interest or get tired quickly, or she may want to play for ages but eat very little. Many babies like to take their time, trying out different pieces of food, moving on, and then coming back to them. All this is normal. Remember that, at this stage, she can still get all the nourishment she needs from breast milk or formula.

Even when she does begin to swallow small amounts, your baby will still spread, smear, and drop a lot of food. Some of this will be on purpose—as a key part of her learning—and some will be by mistake because she is simply not dexterous enough to hold on to it.

Offer your baby three or four different things to start with: maybe a piece of carrot, a broccoli floret, and a large strip of meat (or whatever you happen to be eating that's suitable). Be prepared to have more food ready to offer her or to pick up the food she has dropped and pass it back to her. It may be tempting to restrict your baby to just one piece of food at her first few meals, on the grounds that she isn't going to eat it anyway, but this will be boring for her, and you'll find yourself having to pick the food up to hand back to her every two minutes. It's better to provide a small selection of foods and not worry about whether she eats any of it or not.

On the other hand, it's not a good plan to pile your baby's plate or high chair tray with lots of different foods, either. It's better to start with a small amount and then offer more. Many babies can be overwhelmed by too much choice and quantity in the early stages. Some push all the food away; others focus on one piece of food and throw everything else off the high chair tray; some simply turn away. Watch how your baby responds to food to see how much she can cope with at first.

> **"When we first started, I'd give Etta a plate with lots of food on it, and she'd do this really funny thing: She'd pick up almost every single bit and throw it all behind her until she had just one thing left. She would then grasp it carefully in her hand and start eating. And when she'd eaten it, she'd look around for more. But I couldn't just refill her plate because it'd all go on the floor again. It was as if there was just too much in front of her and she found it confusing. Eventually I worked out that all I had to do was put her food on another plate, and then just offer it to her one or two pieces at a time."**
>
> Julie, mother of Etta, 3 years

As your baby's self-feeding skills develop, you will find that less food is dropped and more is eaten, and you may get a sense of how much she is likely to eat at mealtimes. However, it's only a small step from this to deciding how much she "should" eat, and this is not what BLW is about. Encouraging a child to eat more than she needs is unnecessary and may even be harmful in the long term. At best, it may spoil her enjoyment of mealtimes, and at worst, it could make her more likely to overeat when she's older. It should always be your baby's decision how much she eats; it's her tummy and she knows what she needs. Cleaning the plate

Many of us have grown up being told that it's good manners to finish whatever is on our plates and not to waste food; neither of these things really works for babies or children, and they are often associated with later overeating. It's important not to expect your baby to eat everything she's been given or try to persuade her to eat more than she wants. She should be allowed to eat as much (or as little) as she wants from the food you offer her, so she can choose the nutrients she needs. If she eats everything you've given her, you can offer her some more (or something different) just to make sure she really has had enough; if she turns it down, it's her way of saying she's full. Even though she may have eaten less than you think she should have, she doesn't need you to top her off with something from a spoon; she may well take it to please you, but that doesn't mean she needed it.

> **"I grew up in London during the war, when there was rationing. You couldn't afford to waste food. If I didn't eat up everything I was given, I got it served up again at the next meal. That feeling of needing to finish the plateful (even if I didn't like it) has stayed with me all my life."**
>
> Tony, father of three and grandfather of five

Rejecting Food

If your baby rejects a certain food, it's because she doesn't need it (or want it) at that particular time. It's not a reflection on your cooking, and it doesn't mean she won't eat it if you offer it again. Of course, if she is eating the same food as everyone else, rather than a specially prepared dish, you are much less likely to even notice how much she's eaten—this is another reason why sharing your food with your baby is less stressful for you both than preparing her food separately.

A trick to watch out for!

Occasionally babies tuck away a piece of food—usually in their cheek or the roof of their mouth—only to spit it out or begin chewing it again quite a bit later. This generally happens before they've figured out how to use their tongue to retrieve bits that have become lodged between their gum and their cheek. To be on the safe side, it's probably a good idea, once the meal is over, to check that this hasn't happened before your baby starts playing or has a nap. There's no need to poke around inside her mouth or pin her down to have a good look—just make a game of asking her to open her mouth wide (perhaps by getting her to copy you), or, once she can understand a bit more, teach her to check with her own finger that nothing is lurking inside.

Helping Your Baby to Learn

Babies learn by copying, and they love to join in, so it's important that you eat with your baby whenever possible and offer her some of the same food that you are eating. In fact, you may find she prefers what's on your plate to what's on her own anyway, even if it's exactly the same! (This is probably her instinctive way of checking that the food is safe; see page 36.) Talk to her about the different foods, naming them and describing their colors and textures, so that she learns new words at the same time as she is developing new eating skills.

> **"Meena knows what a piece of carrot is; it's not just orange mush. We talk about the food, and she's getting to know the names of different vegetables. I'll say, 'Where's the cauliflower?' and she'll pick it up. It's great. Babies don't have the chance to learn about real food when you mush it all up into a purée."**
>
> Deepti, mother of Meena, 10 months

Learning by copying involves watching and then doing—and making mistakes. It's important to let your baby find her own way to manage food and not give her more help than she actually needs. Helping her too much (or interfering), criticizing her, laughing, or being frustrated with her will confuse her and may keep her from trying. On the other hand, she doesn't need to be praised when she gets it right, either. After all, she doesn't see a dropped piece of food as a failure, or food eaten as a success—to her it's all just an interesting part of the experiment.

Trying to help or guide your baby can also be distracting for her; she is concentrating on learning about food and how to eat it. If she needs your help, she'll let you know. Most babies really do just want to work out how to do it on their own.

> **"At first, Jamal would be in the process of picking something up and we would reach over to help him when he couldn't quite manage—but you could see his concentration breaking the minute we did it. He was much happier if we just let him do it himself."**
>
> Simon, father of Jamal, 8 months

As we've seen in Chapter 2, babies who are learning how to manage food often gag in the early days. Some may even vomit a little. Although this may look alarming, provided your baby is sitting upright there's usually no need to intervene. In fact, trying to help while she is dealing with the problem is likely to make things more difficult for her. It's best to simply stay calm and be reassuring. She'll naturally stop gagging after a few weeks, once she has learned how to avoid it.

If you think of these early mealtimes not as times for eating but rather as opportunities for learning, you will see that there is no reason to limit them to one, two, or even three a day or to stick to a particular schedule. In fact, the more opportunities your baby has to explore food and to practice with it, the more quickly she will discover what it's all about and develop the self-feeding skills she'll need later.

Dealing with frustration

Some babies seem to go through a period shortly after they start exploring solids when they appear frustrated; it's as though their skills aren't developing fast enough for them. It's tempting to assume that a baby who gets upset and angry is frustrated because she's hungry, but, in the early weeks, if she *is* hungry it is almost certainly for a milk feeding, not for solids. A baby's frustration isn't a sign that she needs her parents to help her by mashing the food up and spooning it into her. Giving food from a spoon may appear to solve the problem, but only because the baby is temporarily distracted. If she is hungry or tired, it's better to offer her a milk feeding or encourage her to have a nap.

Babies can also get frustrated in the first few weeks of BLW simply because they can't do everything they would like to be able to do with the food, in the same way that a new toy can be challenging. Often the problem is that the food is not the right shape or is too slippery for them and needs to be prepared differently, to make it easier to hold (see pages 129–38). The good news is that although a period of frustration seems to be quite common among BLW babies, it rarely lasts more than a week or so, in the same way that being frustrated with a new toy doesn't last forever.

Allowing enough time

Babies need to take their time when they are learning, so it's important not to rush them. It could easily take your baby forty minutes to finish a meal in the early days—it's all about her needing to practice each new skill over and over again as she perfects it.

Allowing babies time to chew thoroughly also helps with digestion (see page 32) and enables them to recognize when they are full, both of which are important for long-term health.

Some babies like to leave pieces of food while they explore other things, but they may want to come back to them later. Grazing like this is quite common, so try to resist the temptation to start cleaning up too soon or nibbling at your baby's food yourself.

Standing back and letting your baby explore may be the hardest part of BLW, but if you can be relaxed about it, you'll soon find this stage doesn't last forever. In fact, the more time you give her to learn how to deal with food—to sniff it, feel it, and play with it—the more quickly she'll become a confident and skilled eater.

> **"Ivor will happily feed himself in his own time. Sometimes he'll sit there for a long time and not do much, and then suddenly eat quite a bit. And some days he'll eat loads and then have nothing but milk for a few days. We really have to trust him and not interfere."**
>
> Amanda, mother of Ivor, 8 months

No pressure

Some babies can be discouraged from trying foods if they are made to feel self-conscious or under pressure by their parents (or others) watching every mouthful they eat. Try not to pay too much attention to your baby while she's eating; you may be fascinated to watch, but she may not feel comfortable being stared at, and it could be distracting for her. Mealtimes should be a normal, enjoyable, everyday activity. Your quiet support and the rewards of handling and eating food are all she needs to grow in skill and confidence.

> **"I remember having dinner with friends when Enrico was about seven or eight months and they were just staring at him eating—they seemed really anxious. I could tell it was really off-putting for him, but I guess it was just all new to them."**
>
> Angela, mother of Enrico, 2 years

Eating Together

Eating together as a family is ideal because your child will learn about more than just how to handle food. She'll learn about taking turns, conversation, and table manners. But organizing mealtimes for a busy family can be a real challenge, especially if you work long hours outside the home. However, the most important thing is that, as much as possible, your baby shouldn't be the only one eating. So even if a family meal isn't feasible, try to make sure that she always eats with at least one other person. If your baby is cared for by someone else, explaining this to her day care or nanny will help to make sure that she experiences shared mealtimes even when she isn't with you.

Breakfast can be rushed in many households, especially if you need to get to work or there are older children to be taken to school or nursery. Many babies won't be interested in breakfast in the early days, but once they are, they tend to be very adaptable: They don't mind if it's not the "right" time to eat. So your baby could have breakfast with you after the school drop-off or when she's at day care. If you are not out at work, lunch is probably the easiest meal to share with her at first. It doesn't have to be anything elaborate, as long as it's nutritious and has a bit of variety in it (see pages 200–02 for ideas).

Shared evening meals are often the most difficult to manage for families. Some parents bring their own mealtime forward, while others rethink their baby's bedtime so that they can all eat together. An alternate solution on working days is for the main caretaker to eat a mini-meal with the baby and another when their partner comes home.

Bear in mind that your baby doesn't need her mealtimes at regular intervals in the early days, because she's not relying on them to satisfy her hunger. It's only as she begins to eat more and discovers that food can stop her from feeling hungry that you'll start to see a pattern in her eating; this is when you can begin to plan how to make more of your family meals coincide with her needs.

Shared meals are probably easiest around a table, but they don't have to be. If you normally eat dinner on your lap in front of the TV, just turn the TV off (so your baby can concentrate, and you can chat) and pull her chair up beside you. Some families like to eat together on a mat or rug on the floor, or you could have a picnic outside.

Aim to treat your baby with the same respect you would show other family members, allowing her to make her own decisions about what to eat and how much. Resist the temptation to wipe her face between mouthfuls or do the dishes while she is still eating.

> "Leah will eat and chew better when I'm eating at the table with her. She watches me the whole time and copies my chewing action. Occasionally I'll get up and start doing something else, and she definitely loses her focus."
>
> Emily, mother of Leah, 7 months

BLW STORY

Once Owen could sit up properly I sat him on my lap at the table with us; he was just over six months. He picked pieces of food up right away but he missed his mouth nearly all the time at first—I don't think he got anything at all for a few days.

But his hand-eye coordination and the way he can get things to his mouth have really changed, even though he only started a couple of weeks ago. The first thing I gave him was some pear—that's what the other kids were eating—and every time he grabbed it, the pear just kept slipping out of his hand; he didn't get any of it. The next time he had pear he kept squeezing it until he eventually worked out the tension he needed to keep it in his hand. After that he started to work out that if he picks up something in his left hand it's easier to pass it to his right hand to get it to his mouth, and now he's started to use his left hand to help to guide it—the left hand pushes the right hand closer to his mouth. It's fascinating.

Actually *eating* stuff still seems to be a bit of a fluke. Food seems to be for the experience of tasting and experimenting rather than for eating at the moment.

It feels great being able to trust my baby's instincts. He doesn't always want food; at dinnertime he's often too tired to be interested, and sometimes I don't give him much at breakfast if I'm late getting the others to school; I'm fairly relaxed with it. But there's no way I could sit and have a meal now and not include him—I'm really enjoying it.

> Sharing normal family meals with Owen makes sense to me; it's so much easier than when I did purées with my first two. In hindsight, Theo (my second) wasn't ready for food until he was about seven months. He didn't like soft food, and he didn't like being fed—he would just spit it all out. He really didn't want to eat much until he was allowed to feed himself. It just seems more natural to let them do that from the start.
>
> **Sam, mother of Ella, 8; Theo, 5; and Owen, 8 months**

Expect Mess

Babies don't understand the concept of mess. Your baby will drop or throw her toys all the time; it's how she learns about gravity, distance, and her own strength. Food is just another toy at first, so babies experiment with it in the same way. To their delight, they find that nothing they have been allowed to handle so far can be squished and spread in quite this way (paint and Play-Doh are usually reserved for toddlers in case the little ones eat it!).

Sometimes the mess is just because young babies' skills are still immature. They often knock something over or push it to one side as they try to pick it up. And because they aren't able to open their fists consciously at first, they tend to drop things by accident when their interest is taken by something else. The most important thing to remember when you are watching your baby happily throwing food over the edge of her high chair is that she doesn't know it matters! She doesn't understand that it needs to be cleaned up—she is just engaged in the important activity of learning. The more relaxed you can be, the faster she will learn.

Minimizing wasted food

There is always some wasted food when babies start on solids, even with purées. If you make your own purée, some will inevitably be lost inside the food blender, while buying commercial baby foods usually means spending money on larger portions than your baby needs. And some food will end up in the high chair or on the floor, however you feed your baby.

BLW is based on sharing your own meals, so it won't make much difference to your food bill. Plus, as your baby starts to recognize familiar foods and become more skilled at handling them, she'll have less need to experiment with squishing and dropping. In the meantime, here are some tips for keeping waste to a minimum:

- Make all your meals something that your baby can share.
- Give your baby only a few pieces of food to explore at a time; if you overload her, she's likely to want to clear the deck just so she can concentrate.
- Make sure that dropped food lands on a clean surface, so you can hand it back to your baby.

As your baby's skills develop and she begins to eat more purposefully, the mess will quickly lessen. In fact, parents who've taken a baby-led approach to complementary feeding often comment on how short lived the messy stage was and how quickly their baby's skills developed. It's also worth remembering that while BLW may be more messy than spoon-feeding during the meals themselves, it's much less messy (and fussy) during the preparation phase, with no blenders or extra bowls to clean.

Mess is an inevitable and important part of babies' learning—trying to fight it is like standing on the seashore and asking the tide not to come in! The secret to coping with the mess is to prepare for it in advance. This means thinking about how you will dress your baby (and yourself!) for her self-feeding adventures and about how best to protect the area around her. It also means making sure meals aren't rushed, giving your baby lots of opportunities to practice, and allowing plenty of time for cleaning up.

> "Mealtimes have been Milo's messy play. He's learned about texture and volume and pouring things through handling food, and it's really helped with hand-eye coordination. Kids love playing with messy stuff. At day care you see kids playing with big trays of colored jelly or cooked spaghetti—but not for their dinner. It's their playtime! It's cutting-edge early learning. Amazing, isn't it?'
>
> Helen, mother of Lizzie, 7 years;
> Saul, 5 years; and Milo, 2 years

> "I really took to 1950s-housewife-style aprons when Justin started BLW, and I haven't looked back. If the baby sits on your lap at mealtimes, you get covered—aprons take all the mess!"
>
> Louise, mother of Justin, 23 months

Fruit stains

Watch out for fruit stains. When babies eat fruit (especially whole fruit), they tend to suck and munch for ages, and the juice or pulp often dribbles down their chin and hands and onto their clothes. You may not notice it at the time, but some fruits, such as banana and apple, can leave very dark stains. You might need to get these items in the laundry quickly!

"After the meal, grab a clean, damp cloth: You clean the baby's face and the baby's hands, and you put him somewhere clean. Then you flip the cloth around and you clean the table: You sweep all the food down onto the floor, then you clean the high chair and sweep all the bits onto the floor. So you've got a big pile on the floor—basically the remains of the entire dinner. You sweep it all up with the cloth, put it into the trash, then put the cloth in the wash. One cloth per meal. Everything's done."

Hazel, mother of Hannah, 8 years; Nathan, 4 years; and Joe, 17 months

Equipment

High chairs

High chairs come in all sorts of shapes and sizes. A high chair with a tray may be useful early on, but one that can be used with the main table will help your baby to feel part of the family meal and to easily reach shared food. In the early months, a small cushion or rolled-up towel around her hips will be all that's needed to keep her steady, but a high chair with a footrest will give her more stability as she gets older.

If you opt for a high chair with a tray, aim for a very wide tray; this usually means less food ends up on the floor. Choose one with a rim around the edge—a tray with no lip may look good, but the food won't stay on it for very long. It's also important to make sure the tray isn't too high in relation to the seat: If your baby's chest is level with the tray, she won't be able to reach the food easily (imagine trying to eat off a table that came up to your armpits!). High chairs with an adjustable-height tray are good, but if you don't have one, putting a folded towel under your baby's bottom will help her until she grows a bit.

High chairs that clamp onto the table can be useful for eating out or traveling but probably aren't comfortable enough for everyday use. Some high chairs can also be used in a low position, which may be handy if you don't eat around a standard table. Chairs that can be adjusted as your child grows are expensive initially but will save you from having to buy a booster seat or a stool when your baby is a toddler. Some can even be used by older children or adults.

Beware of high chairs with lots of padding—they may look more comfortable than plain wood or plastic, but they are much more difficult to clean. And, honestly, you *will* need to clean it. It's also important that your baby's high chair has straps to secure her—and that you use them every time she's in it; she may not be trying to climb out yet, but accidents can happen when even quite young babies wriggle around.

High chairs are handy, but if your baby isn't happy in one, don't force her—she'll be able to eat just as well sitting on your lap and may feel safer there. She'll probably come around to a high chair eventually.

> "If I had another baby I wouldn't do mealtimes any differently—except maybe forget about the high chair! It's so recently that Aidan's sat in a high chair without a fuss—and he's two. So we just decided not to bother because he didn't like it. I just accepted that he would be on my lap rather than have a fight over it. It can be hard to cut food up when he's squirming around, but apart from that, we enjoy it."
>
> Sue, mother of Aidan, 2 years

Floor protection

Carpets and floors can be protected by a large splash mat that's easy to clean, so that any food that gets dropped or thrown can be given back to the baby. A plastic or cotton tablecloth, picnic mat, or even a shower curtain will do fine.

> "We tried a splash mat, but the plastic was fairly thin so we couldn't just mop it to get it clean, we'd have to be down on our hands and knees. In the end we decided to use a cheap cotton tablecloth—then we could just shake it over the trash after a meal and shove it in the washing machine. We ended up needing two or three, so there was always a clean one, but there's always so much laundry with a baby it didn't seem to make any difference."
>
> Ruth, mother of Lola, 19 months

Bibs

A bib will help protect your baby's clothes but bear in mind she may need to reach right out to grab what she wants. A long-sleeved bib (or a toddler's painting apron) will keep her arms clean, but it may get in her way. Pelican bibs are useful for catching dropped food, but some tend to restrict a young baby's movements so they may not be a good idea at first.

Some parents prefer to let their baby eat in a vest, or even just in a diaper, if it's warm enough; skin is easier to wash than clothes. You might want to leave bath time until after she's eaten! As with high chairs, it's not worth battling if your baby doesn't like bibs—mealtimes should always be enjoyable. Accept that she will probably get food on her face, in her hair, and on her clothes and that some will inevitably find its way onto the seat of her high chair or the floor; it's all part of the experience for her.

Plates and cups

Many parents find that it's easier not to bother with a plate at first. A baby of six months is likely to be just as interested in the plate as the food—especially if it's a colorful one designed for babies—and, while this doesn't really matter, it will probably mean that any food on the plate quickly ends up on the floor or in the high chair. And your baby won't remember to put pieces of food back onto the plate after she has tried them, so the area around it will have food on it anyway.

There is no reason why your baby can't eat straight off her high chair tray, or off the tabletop, as long as it's clean (a quick wipe with a clean cloth and a mild detergent is probably all you need). Alternatively, you could put a large rubber place mat or kitchen tray on the table in front of her. Some rubber mats come with pockets that help to contain the mess.

If you do want to use a plate, you may find that a heavy one will be less easy for your baby to lift up—although it will do more damage if she does manage it. Suction plates that stick to the table can be useful, but they tend to catapult out any food left in them when *you* pick them up! There's no need to choose a special child's plate with separate compartments—in fact, this may even give your baby the idea that different foods shouldn't touch each other (a problem that can make mealtimes challenging later).

You're unlikely to need to give your baby a cup at mealtimes at first, since she will still be having her usual milk feedings. Bowls, too, aren't likely to be needed until she can manage runny foods (see pages 136–37). Any plates, bowls, and cups you do use should be clean, but they don't need to be sterilized.

If you want to protect your tabletop, an easy-to-clean plastic tablecloth is a practical option, but it's best to choose one without a busy or colorful pattern, since that may make it harder for your baby to see and recognize the food. It's also important to make sure she can't pull the tablecloth (and everything on it) into her lap or onto the floor.

BLW STORY

About a month ago, James started making it clear that he wanted to sit at the table with us—he wasn't content to sit and watch our mealtimes from a bouncy chair anymore. Some people say when they're interested at mealtimes, they're ready to eat, but I don't think he was hungry, he just wanted to join in, in the same way that he gets frustrated and wants to copy when he sees other babies crawling.

At first, he was interested in things *to do* with mealtimes, but not actually the food. That's really changed in the last two weeks. He's sitting really sturdily now, and he wants more than just a spoon to play with or something nice to suck—he wants to grab things.

He grabbed a piece of cucumber a few weeks ago, but he couldn't hold it well and he dropped it. And the other kids are naughty, they want to give him food. He was given a carrot stick, and a bit of banana, and a mouthful of yogurt by his brother. He managed to grab an apple core to suck on when we were on a picnic the other day and he was very happy with that. And I've had a tomatoey finger that he's sucked on. So he's enjoying tastes. It feels to me like he's ready to eat now.

So, today, I actually offered him something for the first time. It was a nice ripe pear—and he really loved it. I think he was very glad to finally be allowed to eat what he wanted to eat, rather than me saying, "Oh, no, you're not quite old enough yet."

> Last night I made a chicken and bean stew, and I was thinking: *How would this work with James?* But I guess he would maybe have to scoop some up with his hands or grab pieces of chicken. It would be a terrible mess, and I'd just have to get used to it! I think that's my challenge.
>
> **Jane, mother of Rose, 7 years; Edward, 3 years; and James, 6 months**

The Secrets of Successful BLW

- Think of mealtimes as playtimes in the beginning. They are for learning and experimenting, not necessarily for eating.
- Keep giving milk feedings whenever your baby wants, so that her solid foods add to them rather than replacing them. She will reduce the milk feedings gradually, in her own time.
- Eat with your baby and include her in your mealtimes, sharing the same food whenever possible, so that she has plenty of opportunities to copy you and practice her new skills.
- Offer your baby a small selection of foods that are easy for her to pick up. Wedges or stick-shaped pieces of a range of foods and strips of tender meat are all good. Have more ready in case she wants it.
- Don't expect your baby to eat much food at first. Many babies eat very little for the first few months of BLW.

- Expect some mess! Think about how to dress your baby and how to protect the area around her so that dealing with the mess isn't stressful and dropped food can be safely handed back.
- Keep it enjoyable for all of you. By allowing plenty of time and making sure that mealtimes are always relaxed and enjoyable, you will encourage your baby to explore and experiment. That way she'll be eager to try new foods and look forward to mealtimes.

Q&A

My baby is seven months old. My mom is worried that all she does is play with her food. Is this a problem?

Trusting your baby to eat as much as she needs and allowing her to handle or play with her food are two of the most important elements of BLW. They are also the aspects of BLW that many parents (and grandparents) find most difficult to adjust to. As we've seen, for generations parents were encouraged to make sure their babies finished every last bit of food, whether they wanted to or not. Making sure babies put on lots of weight was the goal (see page 91), and playing with food was seen as wasteful and bad behavior.

As your baby gets older, she'll eat more and play less, but she will still need to play with her food sometimes. Allowing a baby the freedom to spend as long as she wants playing with food and not rushing her to eat ensures that her skills develop at the pace that's right for her (see Chapter 2). As her need for food increases, so will her self-feeding skills.

Occasionally an older baby will play with her food because she is bored with that particular food; she may still be hungry but wants (or needs) something new to eat. The easiest way to check is simply to offer her something different, or something from your plate.

Dealing with the doubts of relatives in the early weeks of BLW can be tricky until they are reassured by seeing how well your baby manages food (some of the tips on supporting someone who is looking after your BLW baby may help; see page 187). Have faith in your convictions. Time will show that your instinct to follow BLW is right when your baby turns into a sociable, capable, and enthusiastic mealtime companion who *loves* her grandma's cooking!

> "Once you accept that food is part of their entertainment, not a chore to get through, everything is so much more enjoyable."
>
> Joanne, mother of Caitlyn, 2 years

My baby is five months old and I've been giving her puréed food for a month now. Can I change to BLW?

At five months your baby is almost certainly still too young to feed herself with solid food, although she may be able to pick some pieces up and get them to her lips. Unless you started solids early for a medical reason (in which case you should ask your pediatrician for advice), it might be better to let her go back to full milk feedings for a few more weeks until her system is more mature. Just offer her the chance to feed more often (if you are breastfeeding) or increase the quantity of each feed (if you are formula-feeding) so that you can stop the puréed food. Then, when she reaches six months, you can start with finger foods—just as if she had never had the purées.

If you don't want your baby to stop having solid foods now, you will need to carry on giving her puréed food until she's able to feed herself. You can start offering her foods to hold from about six months, alongside some spoon-feeding. Respond to her cues as much as possible when offering the spoon and wait for her to show you when she's ready to leave purées behind completely.

I've seen mesh feeders advertised for giving babies solid foods. Do they work with BLW?

Mesh feeders are sometimes promoted as a way of allowing babies to munch on "real" food without the risk of choking. They involve a baby chewing on a piece of soft food contained in a plastic net and sucking the food into her mouth when it's mushy enough to pass through the holes. These gadgets are based on a long-established remedy for teething, consisting of a muslin bag filled with ice or frozen breast milk; they have nothing to do with self-feeding or BLW.

As we've seen, provided a baby is upright and in control of her eating, choking is no more of a risk with BLW than with any other method of introducing solids. So claims that a particular product can prevent this risk are misleading. If a baby has a physical or medical condition that prevents her from grasping food and getting it to her mouth, then a mesh feeder may be helpful, but it is neither necessary nor beneficial for a normally developing baby who is able to feed herself with her hands. If a normally developing baby is *not* able to self-feed, she is almost certainly too young to be having solid foods.

Many babies who are given mesh feeders appear to find them frustrating, or simply boring, especially when they realize that the rest of the family doesn't eat this way. Once your baby can sit up and reach for food, she will want to be able to see it and examine its shape and texture, not just taste it. A mesh feeder won't help her learn what real food looks and feels like, nor will it help her work out how to manage foods safely in her mouth. It's simply an unnecessary distraction.

My baby is eight months old and I've been giving her purées up until now. Is it too late to start BLW?

It's never too late to let your baby feed herself at mealtimes. Starting after a few months of spoon-feeding isn't really baby-led weaning in its true sense, but your baby will probably enjoy exploring food if she's given the chance, and she'll still benefit from it. However, she may respond slightly differently from babies who have fed themselves from the beginning.

When babies start BLW at six months, they have a chance to experiment with food and develop self-feeding skills while all their nutrition is still coming from breast milk or formula. This means they can practice feeding themselves before they really need much food. But if they start complementary foods with a period of spoon-feeding and then move on to self-feeding, progress may be less straightforward because this opportunity to learn has been missed.

You may find, when you first offer your baby food to hold, that she gets frustrated because she can't feed herself as fast as she wants to. Babies who have been spoon-fed can get used to swallowing large quantities of food quickly when they are hungry because puréed food doesn't need to be chewed.

Giving your baby the chance to share your mealtimes and feed herself when she *isn't* hungry can help you both avoid this problem, by allowing her to concentrate on discovering that food can be fun without thinking about filling her tummy. You can also start to offer finger foods at her mealtimes alongside her usual purée. As she begins to develop her self-feeding skills, you'll find she is less interested in the purées you offer her, until eventually there will be no need for them.

Some parents find that older babies who are used to being spoon-fed try to cram too much into their mouths when they are allowed to feed themselves. This may be because they haven't had a chance to get used to chewing food before swallowing it, or possibly because they haven't been able to discover how to avoid overfilling their mouths (see pages 62–64). Encouraging self-feeding when your baby isn't hungry is a good way to help her learn not to do this.

However old your baby is when she starts feeding herself, try to give her the chance to join in whenever anyone else is eating. That way she will be encouraged to copy other people and discover the social side of mealtimes. If necessary, just continue to give her the occasional spoonful of puréed food until her self-feeding skills catch up with her appetite.

People keep asking me how much she's having, but I can't really tell because it ends up all over her!

Health professionals, relatives, and friends often ask, "How much is she having?" and many expect parents to say, "Three spoonfuls twice a day," or, "Two whole jars three times a day." BLW is about variety, tastes, textures, and learning, not about the amounts and quantities that most people are familiar with from spoon-feeding, so you might need to have an answer ready for this one!

When babies feed themselves, it can be very difficult, at first, to tell how much they have eaten. Once the baby has spread the food around her high chair tray, lost some under her bottom and dropped bits onto the floor, working out what must have been swallowed is a challenge. And when we are giving babies sticks of food to hold, we aren't measuring it in spoonfuls in the first place. The truth is, it doesn't matter how much your child is eating as long as she is healthy, has plenty of opportunities to eat as much as she needs, and is having as many milk feedings as she wants.

As we've seen, most people's ideas about the amounts babies "should" eat are not realistic. So try not to feel under pressure to gauge how much your baby is eating and instead focus on how much she enjoys mealtimes and the variety of tastes and textures she is able to explore.

> "My grandma asked me the other day how much Leo was having. I said, 'Oh, he's having loads! Carrot, broccoli, chicken, banana, avocado, beans, toast, olives, cheese—everything.' She didn't know what to say!"
>
> Claire, mother of Leo, 8 months

Will, 5 months, has enough coordination to accurately bring objects to his mouth so he can explore them with his lips and tongue.

For Jack, at 6 months, this banana is a completely new thing to be examined—first by touch, sight, and smell, and then by taste.

George, 6 months, is showing he's ready for solid food by grabbing a carrot from his sister's plate.

Joaquim, almost 6 months, is curious about this piece of meat, which may be his first taste of solid food.

Felix, 6 months, is using both hands to guide his toast to his mouth, but he hasn't yet learned which end to hold.

Joaquim, 6 months, has finished exploring his own food and now wants to try some of his brother Benjamin's food.

Owen, 6 months, is working out how to keep hold of a slippery chunk of beet from his mom's salad.

These vegetables are just the right size and shape for a 6-month-old baby like Lilly to manage.

Valentina, 6 months, is fascinated by star fruit—she'll learn about its shape, texture, and taste as she handles it.

At 7 months, Lara finds it helpful to use her fingers to keep some melon in her mouth while she chews.

Laura, 8 months, is discovering that broccoli tips taste and feel different from the stalk.

▲ Jamie, 7 months, and his granddad enjoy lunch together now and then.

◀ George, 7 months, and his mom often share a meal at a local café.

Aidan, 7 months, is discovering how noodles work. ▶

▲ Hannah, 8 months, wants to try some of her dad's falafel in pita bread.

◀ Oscar, 8 months, has worked out how to separate the flesh of his pineapple from the skin.

Robert, at 8 months, is carefully holding his strawberry so that he can take small bites from it. ▶

Although Seren, 9 months, has only two teeth, she has no trouble gnawing her apple. ▶

◀ Caterina, 8 months, holds a piece of watermelon in each hand, munching on each piece in turn.

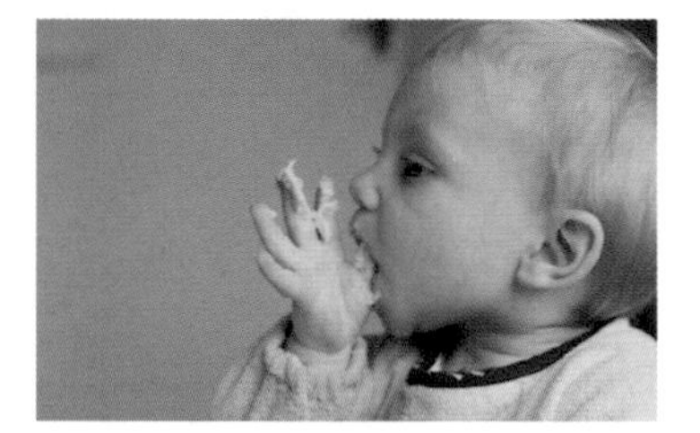

◀ At 10 months, Orban has discovered how to use his fingers to dip into soft foods such as hummus.

Lila, 9 months, can now pick up small pieces of chopped meat with her thumb and forefinger; she concentrates as she puts them in her mouth.

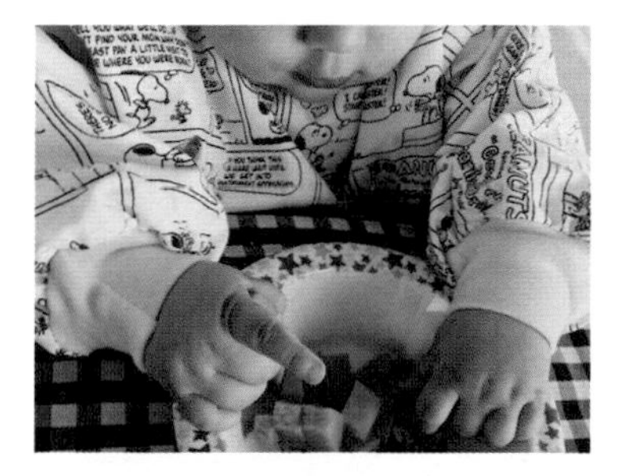

At 9 months, Benjamin is easily able to manage small chunks of food and is no longer distracted by the bowl.

Aidan, 10 months, won't eat this whole lamb chop, but he will get a lot of useful nutrients from gnawing and sucking on it.

Pedro, 11 months, is using both hands to help accurately guide his food to his mouth.

At 10 months, Oscar is confident with a spoon but still finds it helpful to use his hands sometimes.

▲ Charlie, 12 months, practices using a fork as she shares a roast with her family.

Madeleine, 15 months, is digging in to pasta salad at a picnic with family and friends. ▶

◀ By serving himself, Owen, 17 months, is learning to judge volume and distance as well as how to gauge his own appetite.

4 First Foods

> "Within two and a half weeks [of starting BLW], my partner and I sat at the dinner table, eating homemade vegetarian lasagna and peas, as our daughter sat next to us—eating the exact same meal and devouring it with gusto. Was she plastered in it by the end? Yes. Was her high chair filthy? Yes. Was it one of the most amazing things I've ever witnessed? Definitely."
>
> Lisa, mother of Kyla, 11 months

Basic Principles

If you have read any other guides to starting solid foods, you have probably found that many give instructions for the order in which foods should be introduced. However, this advice is outdated. The immune and digestive systems of a six-month-old baby are mature enough to cope with a range of foods, so such restrictions are unnecessary. This is true whether or not a BLW approach is used.

As a general rule, your meals will be fine for your baby to eat if you start with natural ingredients and serve as much fresh food as possible. There are a few things that babies shouldn't have, but there's no need to introduce foods in any particular order or to start with one taste at a time.

Many people assume that the first complementary foods should be plain, steamed vegetables or fruit. Although these will be easy for your baby to handle, he needs to be offered a wider range of nutrients than those foods alone can provide—including, for example, iron and zinc. There's no reason why he can't share a casserole, salad, pasta dish, stir fry, or roast dinner—or any other healthy meal that can be adapted to include shapes that he can hold. You should aim to offer the following:

- Nutritious food
- Food from each of the major food groups at least once a day (see pages 193–95)
- A wide range of foods throughout the week so that your baby gets the chance to sample different tastes and textures
- Sizes and shapes that your baby can manage (bearing in mind that his skills will quickly progress).

You can find more details on nutrients and providing healthy, balanced meals for the whole family in Chapter 6.

Foods to Avoid

Although your baby will probably be able to share most of the food you eat, it's important to know which foods are not good for babies and why they should be avoided, so that your baby's diet is as healthy as possible. The following is a list of the main foods you need to avoid when sharing your meals with your baby. There is more information about them later in this chapter:

- Foods containing added salt. This is probably the most important single ingredient to avoid.
- Foods containing added sugar.
- Foods containing artificial flavorings, colors, preservatives, and sweeteners. Common examples include monosodium glutamate (MSG), aspartame, and other additives, which may have health risks. Generally, the fewer (and more recognizable) the ingredients listed on a packaged food, the better it is.
- Ready meals, processed snacks, and junk food. These are usually high in salt, sugar, hydrogenated fats, and artificial additives.
- Uncooked or lightly cooked seafood (such as mussels or prawns), which can cause serious stomach infections.
- Raw honey, which is best left until your baby is at least a year old, as it has been shown to be a potential source of botulism—another serious infection.
- Shark, swordfish, and marlin, which can contain high levels of pollutants, especially mercury.
- Unpasteurized and mold-ripened cheeses, such as Brie, which may contain listeria.
- Raw bran and bran products.

- Caffeinated drinks, such as tea, coffee, and cola. Caffeine is a stimulant, which can make babies irritable. Tea also interferes with iron absorption.
- Rice milk, which contains arsenic, so shouldn't be given to children under five years.
- Soy milk, which contains high levels of aluminum and plant estrogens.
- Fizzy drinks and undiluted fruit juices, which can cause tooth decay.

Care should also be taken to avoid or adapt foods that pose a choking risk (see page 35), and you may also need to avoid some foods if there is the likelihood of serious allergy (see pages 126–27). Apart from this, you just need to offer your baby a balanced selection of foods—preferably what you're eating yourself—and let him choose what to eat. The greater the range of tastes and textures he is allowed to try (and to refuse) when he is young, the more likely he is to enjoy a wide range of foods later.

Salt

Too much salt is bad for anyone, but it can be dangerous for babies. Their kidneys are not mature enough to deal with too much salt, and it can cause severe illness. It's also better for your baby's long-term health if you can keep salt levels low for him as a child, so he doesn't develop a taste for salty food as he gets older.

Salt is added to many foods to enhance the flavor, especially ready-made meals, store-bought sauces, stocks, and gravies, and it is used as a preservative in foods such as bacon and ham, and many canned foods. Most of the salt we eat is hidden in our food, not added from the saltshaker during cooking or at the table, so avoiding salt means having to think about what to buy as well as how to cook.

Salty foods to avoid if possible

- Prepackaged meals, including ready-to-cook pizza
- Some breakfast cereals (check the information on the box)
- Ultra-processed cheese foods
- Salted snacks, such as chips
- Some jarred pasta or curry sauces
- Sauces such as ketchup, steak sauce, or soy sauce
- Prepackaged gravy and stock cubes (choose low-salt varieties)
- Canned and dried soups
- Smoked meat and fish
- Foods in brine (salt water), such as olives, tuna, or anchovies (choose varieties in water or oil)
- Most takeout foods

Foods to limit to small quantities, occasionally

- Hard cheeses (such as Parmesan, Edam, and cheddar)
- Sausages (especially pepperoni, chorizo, and salami)
- Ham and bacon
- Fresh bakery products such as ciabatta, pastries, and cheese straws

Babies under a year old should have no more than 1 gram of salt (400 milligrams of sodium) per day. Prepackaged meals and processed foods often contain levels of salt that are far too high for babies. Some cheeses, such as Parmesan, feta, and processed cheese (slices, spread, and triangles) can contain over 1 gram of salt per 100 grams (3.5 ounces) of cheese. Some breads can contain 1 gram of salt in a couple of slices. So although cheese and bread can be good foods, they shouldn't be given to babies at every meal. A good rule is to make sure you don't offer your baby more than one salty food per day, and that you provide plenty of nonsalty foods such as fresh vegetables at the same meal, along with water or breast milk to drink.

As with all foods, it's worth reading labels carefully when buying. Some manufacturers list salt as sodium (or Na); multiplying the amount of sodium listed by 2.5 will tell you the equivalent of milligrams of salt. As a general guide, a food is high in salt if it has more than 1.5 grams of salt (600 milligrams of sodium) per 100 grams, while a low-salt food has 0.3 gram or less of salt (120 milligrams or less of sodium) per 100 grams.

Many parents choose to prepare their own food without salt when they have a young baby, so that the baby can join in their meals without risk. Parents often find they can unlearn their own preference for salty foods quite quickly, just by changing what they eat and the way they cook. Using herbs and spices can sometimes satisfy the desire for highly flavored food, and many parents are surprised to find that their baby likes the taste of spicy food.

If you do want to add salt to your own meal, add it at the table rather than during cooking. Bear in mind that, as your baby gets older, he'll start wanting to copy everything you do—so one day he may make a grab for the saltshaker and pour some onto *his* food!

Sugar

Sugar is added to many foods and drinks as a sweetener but it doesn't contain any key nutrients, so it provides only empty calories. It also damages teeth—even before they come in. Starting your baby off on foods that are naturally low in sugar should help to prevent him from developing a craving for highly sweetened foods later in life.

Sugar is often hidden in products such as sauces, breakfast cereals, and flavored yogurts. Even some commercially prepared baby foods have high levels of sugar. Watch out for names such as *sucrose*, *dextrose*, *fructose*, *glucose syrup*, and *corn syrup* on packages and labels—they are all types of sugar.

There is no need to aim for a totally sugar-free diet for your baby. The occasional cake, cookie, or dessert is fine, especially if it's homemade. You can often reduce the amount of sugar you use by adapting recipes—for example, by using naturally sweet dessert apples instead of cooking apples to make an apple pie, or by adding mashed banana or dried fruit to sweeten dishes. Molasses is a nutritious natural sweetener that can also be useful. And in many recipes, halving the amount of sugar makes no difference to whether or not the recipe works.

Foods That Are Different for Babies

While we can all benefit from eating less salt, sugar, and processed foods, babies' needs differ from those of adults in two key areas: fat and fiber.

Fat

Babies and young children need proportionately more fat in their diet than adults because they burn up energy easily. So, if as a family you generally have a low-fat diet, you'll need to make sure you offer your baby some foods that contain plenty of fat. For example, your baby should have full-fat versions of milk, cheese, and yogurt, not reduced-fat or low-fat (but see page 196 for fats to avoid). There's no rush though, for the first few months of solid foods your baby should still be getting most of his nourishment from breast milk or formula, both of which contain good amounts of healthy fat. In fact, breast milk is the best source of the essential fatty acid omega-3, which is especially important for brain development.

Fiber

Most dietary fiber, as found in oats, lentils, peas, and fruit, is good for babies because it helps to keep their bowels healthy. However, it's a good idea to limit the amount of whole grains (for example, whole wheat bread and pasta) your baby is offered. This is because the amount and type of fiber in these foods (see page 194) makes them very filling, meaning he may have no room left for foods with other important nutrients.

This doesn't mean you have to switch to white bread or rice if you normally eat whole wheat bread and brown rice. In fact, it's probably a good idea to get your baby used to whole grain foods early on so that he develops a taste for them, since they tend to be more nutritious than processed foods. You simply need to make sure that he has plenty of other healthy foods to choose from so he can decide how much of the whole grain foods to eat. Some parents alternate brown and white rice, pasta, and bread so that their baby is offered a variety.

Concentrated fiber, such as raw bran or high-fiber cereals, shouldn't be offered to babies because it can irritate their digestive tract and may inhibit the absorption of minerals such as calcium and iron.

Vitamin supplements

In the US, supplementation of vitamin D is recommended for babies and children. This is because it's difficult to get enough vitamin D from sunlight (the ideal source) and it is not easily obtained from food alone. Breastfed babies are generally given supplements in the form of liquid drops, starting at birth. Formula-fed babies don't require additional vitamin D until their intake of formula begins to decrease and reaches less than 1,000 milliliters per day, because formula is already fortified with this vitamin.

Oily fish

Although oily fish is one of the most nutritious foods and contains plenty of the essential fatty acid omega-3, current US guidelines suggest that babies and children should have no more than one portion of oily fish per week because of concerns about mercury levels. Oily fish include sardines, trout, mackerel, and salmon. Fresh tuna also counts as an oily fish, but canned tuna doesn't (the canning process reduces the level of beneficial fats). White fish such as cod, pollock, and haddock are fine to eat more often as they are not classified as oily.

What About Allergies?

For most babies there's no need to delay offering foods that have a reputation for triggering an allergic reaction, since current evidence suggests that this doesn't reduce the chance of them developing an allergy to those foods. On the other hand, breastfeeding—from birth, and while new foods are being introduced—does appear to provide some protection.

However, if there are allergies in your baby's immediate family, it's a good idea to be cautious when introducing solids. The most common culprits are cow's milk, eggs, peanuts, tree nuts, wheat, fish, shellfish, soy, and sesame, but allergies to other foods are also possible.

One of the advantages of baby-led weaning is that it allows babies to try out different foods separately, rather than being presented with them blended together. This can help both of you to identify foods that may cause a problem. Waiting a few days between foods you are concerned about will allow you to spot any potentially allergic reaction. If in doubt, speak to your pediatrician or a pediatric allergist.

Not all reactions to food are caused by an allergy; some are the result of a temporary food intolerance. Many children who have reactions to foods as babies can tolerate those foods by the age of three.

So, even if your baby does react badly to a food, he may not need to avoid it forever. Some babies develop a rash around their mouth when they eat citrus fruits or strawberries. This is most likely a reaction to the high acid content of these foods, but it could be an allergic reaction. If you are unsure, seek medical advice, and trust your baby if he refuses a food. Some parents recall that as babies their children avoided foods that they later turned out to be allergic to.

> **"Oscar tried a strawberry when he was about eight months old, and he got a weird rash on his face. After that, he wouldn't eat them. He squeezes them, squishes them, but he won't eat them."**
>
> Natalie, mother of Oscar, 14 months

As much as possible, try to make sure your baby has a truly varied diet. Think about whether you have developed routines that could lead to him being offered the same limited range of foods every day. Many people have dairy foods and wheat at least twice every day; both are common causes of intolerance and allergy.

BLW STORY

Fern didn't even realize what food was at six months. At seven months, she started to realize that we were eating, but if we put something from our plates in front of her she didn't take much notice. It's only recently that she's trying to get at the food. She'll gnaw on a chicken bone, and if she has a chunk of banana she'll gum it a bit and spit it out and play with it, but she won't necessarily eat it. But at least she's putting it in her mouth. And at ten months, there's really no point in giving her purée on a spoon; it's easier to give her real food and let her work it out for herself.

We've got a lot of allergies in our family, and Fern has had very bad reactions to foods that I've eaten, through my breast milk. We worked out it was prawns, grapes, and pork, and since I've eliminated them she's gotten much better. So I'm trying to introduce basic foods during BLW, just to see how she manages; she's only had banana, avocado, chicken, plantain, and potato. I think being slow to start on solids could be connected to her allergies.

In our family there's another baby, who's only two weeks older than Fern. She started solids at four months and has been on three meals a day for ages, so sometimes there's a bit of comparison between them. Everyone can see that Fern is doing just as well health-wise as the other baby, but they keep asking, "Is she eating yet?" Some of the family are OK with it, but some think I should start force-feeding her. I suppose they think she should be eating what everyone else eats by now. But I think: *When they're ready, they're ready.* And it's not like she's wasting away; she's a big baby.

Sandra, mother of Reuben, 3 years; and Fern, 10 months

Adapting Food in the Early Months

Most foods can be adapted easily so that your baby can eat them, too. As we've seen, to start with it's best to offer large pieces that can be held easily and sucked or chewed. Ironically, bite-sized pieces will probably be hardest for your baby to deal with at first, because he won't be able to get at them once he's closed his hand around them. As his skills develop, remember to offer him new textures alongside something he can manage, so that he can practice new techniques (see pages 154–55).

Meat

Meat is an important first food because it contains plenty of iron and zinc, which are likely to be the first nutrients your baby needs from solid foods. So, unless you wish to bring him up as a vegetarian, meat should be one of his first tastes (see page 197 for alternative sources of iron).

Meat should be cut or torn into long strips or large chunks. Chicken will probably be easiest for your baby to manage at first—chicken legs are best because they're easy to hold and the meat on them is less crumbly than breast meat.

You can also try offering ground meat, perhaps made into patties or mini-burgers. You'll soon find that your baby can manage ground meat in clumps surprisingly well with his fingers, too.

Red meat can be made more tender by stewing rather than roasting. You can also make meat such as pork, beef, or lamb easier for your baby to chew by cutting it across, rather than along, the fibers. For poultry (chicken, turkey, duck, etc.), it's best to divide the meat along the fibers, otherwise it tends to be too crumbly to hold.

Pre-chewing

It's traditional in some cultures to pre-chew food for babies, to soften it and mix it with saliva so that it is easier to digest. The food is then either passed directly from the mother's mouth to the baby's as a sort of kiss or is offered to the baby by hand. Pre-chewing is most often done with meat, to break down the fibers so that the baby can manage it more easily. There is no reason why BLW parents shouldn't do this, but it doesn't seem to be really necessary. Although young babies can't easily chew meat (especially red meat), they can get a lot of goodness from just sucking on it. In particular, sucking provides them with the meat juices, which are rich in iron. If someone else chews the meat first, the baby may get more of the meat protein, but he could lose out on some of the iron.

Eggs

Eggs are very nutritious. They can be made into firm omelets or frittatas and cut into fingers or chunks, or your baby may enjoy bringing soft handfuls of scrambled eggs to his mouth. He might also enjoy dipping toast fingers (or his own fingers!) into a boiled or poached egg. However, unless they are pasteurized, eggs should be cooked until the yolk and white are solid, to avoid the risk of *salmonella* poisoning.

Vegetables and fruit

Vegetables that are hard when raw should be cut into a stick or finger shape (rather than round slices) and cooked (without salt) so that they are soft but not soggy. Al dente may be fine for you, but remember that your baby doesn't have much in the way of teeth. Boiling or steaming is good, but a tasty alternative is to roast sticks of vegetables in the oven. This gives them a slightly crisp coating and makes them easier to grip. Bear in mind that some vegetables, such as carrots, sweet potatoes, and parsnips shrink when roasted, so cut extra-wide finger shapes. Sticks of softer vegetables, such as cucumber, can be offered raw.

> **"The first time I gave Callum carrot sticks, they weren't steamed enough so he just sucked on them, and they got smoother and smoother. It took me a while to realize he just needed them to be steamed for a few minutes more than ours, so he could actually munch them."**
>
> Ruth, mother of Callum, 18 months

Large fruits, such as melon and papaya, can be cut into stick shapes or wedges, while small round ones (such as grapes) should be cut in half. Berries such as blueberries are likely to be too small for your baby to pick up for a while, but you can offer them slightly squashed, so he can try grabbing them. Plums can be cut into quarters. Apples, pears, peaches, and nectarines can be offered whole or in wedges. Apples are easier to gnaw (and less likely to snap unexpectedly) when they are slightly soft than when they're really crisp. Wedges of very crisp apple can be softened easily in a microwave.

It's best to leave some of the skin on most fruit and vegetables to make them easier to hold—at least until your baby is able to bite pieces off. Apples, pears, avocados, mangos, and potatoes all work well with some skin left on. Your baby will soon work out how to scrape the flesh with his teeth or gnaw it with his gums. Some babies manage oranges best as large wedges while others prefer to handle individual segments (with pithy strings removed).

Easy first finger foods for babies

- Steamed or lightly boiled whole vegetables, such as green beans, baby corn, snow peas or sugar snap peas
- Steamed or lightly boiled florets of cauliflower or broccoli
- Steamed, roasted, or stir-fried vegetable sticks, such as carrot, potato, eggplant, sweet potato, rutabaga, parsnip, zucchini, or winter squash
- Raw sticks of cucumber. These are ideal for babies who are teething—fridge-cold cucumber is soothing for their gums
- Thick slices of avocado (not too ripe or it will be very squishy)
- Strips of firm omelet
- Chicken (as a strip of meat or on a leg bone)
- Thin strips of beef, lamb, or pork
- Fruit, such as soft apple, pear, banana, peach, nectarine, or mango—either whole or as sticks
- Plain rice cakes or fingers of toast—on their own or with a homemade spread, such as sardine and tomato or cottage cheese
- Homemade meatballs or beef burgers
- Homemade lamb or chicken nuggets
- Homemade fish cakes or fish fingers
- Homemade falafel or lentil patties

Remember, you don't need to choose recipes specifically designed for babies; use your favorite recipes but be careful to keep salt and sugar to a minimum.

Many parents offer bananas with some skin on, too: Wash the skin first (in case it gets chewed), then trim it so there is an inch or so of banana sticking out and it looks like an ice-cream cone. Once your baby is more skilled, let him try the banana skinless, to work out how much pressure he can use before he squishes it completely!

The following tips may be helpful:

- Crinkle-cutters can be useful for cutting fruit and vegetables to make them easier for a baby to grip.
- Taking a bite out of a whole fruit before you give it to your baby will make it easier for him to get started.
- It can be handy to keep some extra portions of vegetables prepared in the freezer, just in case you decide to eat something that you don't want your baby to share.
- Mashed vegetables make a good not-too-runny sauce to serve with pasta.

Bread

Bread can be a good finger food, but babies under a year old shouldn't have more than two slices a day because it tends to be high in salt. Most breads are easier for young babies to cope with if they are toasted; white bread, in particular, becomes quite doughy once it's wet and can be difficult to manage in the mouth—especially when it's very fresh. Flat breads, such as tortillas, pitas, and naan, are less crumbly so may be easier for your baby to handle at first.

Low-salt breadsticks are handy for dipping into soft foods such as hummus; they can be given to your baby already loaded until he is able to dip for himself. Salt-free rice cakes are a good alternative to bread, particularly for spreading with soft food or a thick sauce.

Pasta

Pasta twists (fusilli), shells, and bows are less slippery and easier to grip than smoother shapes; your baby will probably find most pasta easier to manage plain, without any sauce at first. Try offering some with sauce and some without so he can try both.

> **"To start with, we gave Maria pieces of well-steamed carrot, bits of pear or apple, or chunks of chicken or lamb—whatever was for dinner. She had broccoli quite early, which she loved. She'd just suck on it like a lollipop—now she's chewing the top off and getting a lot down."**
>
> Alison, mother of Maria, 7 months

Rice

Rice is a good, nutritious base for a meal, but parents sometimes find they need to adapt the way they cook it or the type of rice they use to make it easier for their baby to manage.

Many rices, such as Thai rice, Japanese sushi rice, and risotto rice, are naturally sticky and easy to grab in handfuls. Other rices, such as Basmati, are easier for babies to handle if they are either slightly overcooked or cooked the day before they're eaten (see page 229 for important safety information about storing rice).

Adapting foods that pose a choking risk

Some foods are risky for babies because of their shape or consistency. Most can be adapted to make them safer, but others should be avoided completely until your child is older. Here's what to do:

- Remove pits from fruits such as cherries, olives, and plums.
- Small round fruits, such as grapes and cherry tomatoes, should be cut into halves or quarters.
- Very crisp or hard fruits (such as apple) can be softened in a microwave.
- Thin bones, skin, and gristle should be removed from meat.
- Check fish carefully for bones.
- Coin-shaped pieces, such as round slices of carrot or sausage, should be avoided or cut in half.
- Take care with cakes, casseroles, and salads that may contain small, hard pieces of food.
- Whole nuts (or large pieces) should be avoided until your child is at least three years old. Nuts can easily get lodged in a small child's windpipe and, unlike other foods, do not dissolve. (It's OK to offer ground nuts or nut butters to your baby.)

However, all babies will eventually find a way of dealing with rice: Some simply put their face quite close to the plate and shovel the rice in; others enjoy practicing their pincer grip by selecting one grain at a time. It's a bit slow, but a lot of fun—and very good for hand-eye coordination!

Runny foods

Runny foods such as yogurt and oatmeal may seem impossible for your baby to eat without spoon-feeding, but babies are remarkably adaptable and will quickly find their own way to manage them. These tips may help:

- Smooth, runny yogurts can be drunk straight from the container.
- Oatmeal can be made a little thicker than usual. Your baby may be able to get soft handfuls into his mouth.
- Soup is easier to manage if it has lumps that can be fished out.
- Smooth or thin soup can be thickened with rice or pieces of bread. You can also offer bread or rice cakes for your baby to dip in the soup.
- Some babies can manage a spoon when it is given to them to hold ready-loaded, even though they aren't yet able to load it without help. If you don't want your baby to wave the spoon around or turn it upside down and lose all the food, you can hold the spoon yourself, allowing him to hold your hand and guide it to his mouth so he is still in control.

- You can offer your baby other foods, such as breadsticks or cooked carrot sticks, to dip into soft or runny food (see the next section), or he may just prefer to use his fingers.

> "I made a thick split pea and ham soup, and Fay absolutely loved it. I gave her a spoon, and she dipped it in and sucked it a bit. But in the end, she abandoned the spoon and just put her face in the bowl. (We used a suction bowl, but I had to hold the top of it so she didn't tip it completely upside down.) After that she put her hands in and seemed to get an enormous amount of soup. That was one of the first really successful things. And that was relatively early on; she was probably less than seven months when we did that."
>
> Janice, mother of Alfie, 4 years; and Fay, 8 months

Dips and dippers

Most babies can dip from about nine months, but as with everything, some will be able to do it much earlier (or later) than others. Using a dipper can be a lot of fun. It means your baby can eat soft or runny food such as yogurt and oatmeal without the need for a spoon, and it's also a good way for him to acquire the skills needed for using a spoon later. He may discover dipping for himself with any piece of food that works—be ready for some odd combinations, such as a finger of roasted carrot dipped into pudding!

Of course, if you like dipping, too, there are lots of traditional dips that can be made easily at home—for example, hummus, guacamole, tzatziki, and baba ghanoush.

Ideas for dippers

- Pieces of tortilla, naan, pita bread, or toast
- Breadsticks, oat cakes, or plain rice cakes (salt- and sugar-free)—these may be easier to dip if they are broken in half first
- Wedges of fruit, such as nectarine or mango
- Thick sticks of raw vegetable, such as celery (tough strings removed), peppers, zucchini, and cucumber
- Cooked whole baby corn or green beans
- Roasted vegetable fingers, such as carrots, butternut and other squash, parsnip, zucchini, potatoes, and sweet potatoes

Drinks

How soon your baby starts to need a drink with his meals depends to some extent on whether you are breastfeeding or formula-feeding. Fully breastfed babies can get everything they need in the way of food and drink, even in very hot weather, just by deciding how often to feed and for how long, because breast milk changes throughout a feed (from more thirst-quenching to more filling). This process can continue working well when your baby is having solid foods, too, provided he is allowed to breastfeed whenever he wants to. If you also give him the chance to have a drink of water with his meals, he will learn about it in just the same way as he learns about food.

What about milk?

In the past it was thought that babies and young children needed lots of cow's milk to be well-nourished, but they don't need any drinks other than water or breast milk. There's nothing magic about cow's milk. In fact, in many cultures it's normal not to eat or drink any animal milk or dairy products.

All animal milks are designed to provide the baby animal of that species with all the nutrients they need, in the right proportions. The only milk that can do this for human babies is human breast milk. Cow's milk (and milk from goats and sheep) is too filling for babies to have as a drink and can dull their appetite so that they don't eat enough other foods. This may make a baby anemic or otherwise undernourished. Animal milk is also a common allergy trigger. However, milk is a good source of protein, calcium, fat, and vitamins A, B, and D, so it can be a useful part of a baby's diet. The key is to treat it as food, rather than as a drink, and to use it only in cooking or with breakfast cereals until your baby is over a year old.

Formula is too rich to be really thirst-quenching and doesn't change throughout the feed, so formula-fed babies need to be offered drinks of water occasionally even before they start on solids. Offering your baby water regularly, preferably in an open cup, will help him (and you) to recognize when he is thirsty rather than hungry.

Water and breast milk are the best drinks for babies and young children. Tap water is fine—preferably filtered—and it doesn't need to be boiled once the baby is over six months old. If you offer your baby fruit or vegetable juice, dilute it with at least ten parts water to one part juice, and bear in mind that even diluted juice contains sugar that can damage growing teeth. It can also fill a baby up and take the place of more nourishing food.

Breakfast

Parents new to BLW often wonder what they can offer their baby for breakfast. But many babies aren't interested in eating breakfast to start with—at that time of day they just want to snuggle up and have a milk feeding. Once your baby does start to take an interest, the following tips and ideas may be useful:

- Babies can often manage mushy things such as breakfast cereal and milk fairly well with their fingers if they're allowed to practice, so your baby may be able to share what everyone else is eating.
- Remember to allow plenty of time—breakfast can be rushed in many households, and babies need time, both to experiment with food and to eat.
- Offer your baby plenty of variety throughout the week (many adults get into the habit of having the same breakfast every day).

Breakfast ideas

- Fresh fruit.
- Homemade oatmeal: While cooking you can add stewed or grated apples or pears, blackberries, blueberries, raisins, apricots, dates, cranberries, or figs. If using dried fruit, either presoak it or make sure it is cooked long enough to be soft. Fruit purée, freshly ground nuts or sunflower seeds, strawberries, or a little molasses can be added at the table. Although oatmeal is usually made from oats, it can also be made with rice flakes, millet flakes, or quinoa flakes (available in health food shops and in many supermarkets).
- Live, full-fat natural yogurt with fresh fruit. (Babies and toddlers often love stirring berries or stewed or puréed fruit into their yogurt, or dipping pieces of fruit into it.)
- Scrambled egg.
- Cereal, with or without milk: Some babies love dry cereal; others prefer it mushy. Avoid cereals coated in chocolate, honey, or sugar, as well as high-fiber, bran-based cereals. Choose varieties that are low in salt and sugar.
- Pancakes: These are easy to make. They can be spread with stewed or grated apple or pear, or pieces of soft fruit, and offered cut up into strips.
- Toast, oat cakes, or plain rice cakes spread with nut butter, cream cheese, or 100 percent fruit spread.

Easy Snacks and Food on the Move

Once your baby starts to rely on solid foods to fill his tummy, it's a good idea to make sure you have a healthy snack with you when you go out together, just in case he gets hungry before you get home. The following are a few ideas for foods that are easy to carry with you.

- Fruit (especially varieties that are not too fussy, such as soft apples, pears, and bananas)
- Tomatoes, sticks of cucumber, peppers, or celery (with tough strings removed)
- Cold cooked vegetables (carrots, broccoli, etc.)
- Cold cooked baby corn or corn on the cob
- Sandwiches
- Pasta, with or without sauce, or pasta salad
- Yogurt—plain, full-fat, live yogurt is best, maybe with fresh fruit added (flavored yogurts often contain a lot of sugar)
- Guacamole or hummus, with breadsticks, chunky carrot sticks, etc.
- Low-salt oat cakes, rice cakes, or toast—spread with nut butter, cream cheese, or sugar-free fruit spread
- Dry, low-sugar breakfast cereal

Remember to read labels carefully. Teething cookies and many prepackaged snacks aimed at children tend to contain lots of sugar and additives and are best avoided.

Food in pouches

Pouches are often seen as a convenient snack option for babies and toddlers when families are out and about, but, like mesh feeders (see pages 112–13), they may be a source of frustration for BLW babies. The baby can't see the food, explore it, or touch it with his hands, and he can't bite or chew it, either. So he may react with suspicion because he can't tell if the food is something he's had before or whether it's even safe to eat.

Many pouches contain a combination of flavors, meaning that the baby can't select the foods he wants or needs. It's also difficult for him to predict or control how the food goes into his mouth: If he squeezes too hard (or if someone else squeezes the pouch), the food could go too far back, putting him at risk of choking.

All in all, pouches aren't a good option for a baby who wants to feed himself.

Desserts

There are plenty of nutritious desserts you can offer your baby, but there is no need to offer them every day. Having a sweetened dessert with every meal, even if it's just a yogurt, will encourage him to develop a sweet tooth and may mean he begins to expect a dessert every time. His taste buds are being programmed during these formative first years of eating, and you can help him to develop good (or bad) eating habits that will last a lifetime. Having a dessert at every meal can also make it all too easy to slip into a "finish your vegetables and then you can have dessert" scenario, especially if your baby likes to take his time over his main course.

If, as a family, you usually have a dessert, go for a healthy (preferably homemade) one wherever possible. Even commercially made "healthy options" often have high levels of artificial sweeteners and additives. Bear in mind that if everyone else is eating something, your baby will want to try it, too—so if you don't want him eating an unhealthy dessert, either have it after he's gone to bed or see if you can offer him something that looks almost identical (this doesn't always work!). However, if you make your dessert as nutritious as your main course, then you won't have to worry if, occasionally, your baby eats only the sweet dish.

Ideas for healthy desserts

- Fresh fruit
- Homemade fruit salad
- Plain, full-fat live yogurt with fresh or stewed fruit
- Homemade rice pudding
- Apple pie (made with sweet dessert apples rather than cooking apples so you don't need to add much sugar)
- Baked pears or apples

"We don't tend to eat too many sweet things at home, but if I'm out for a meal and I have a dessert, then Mila will share it. I don't believe in not letting her have things that I'm having, because it seems hypocritical. Of course, I probably shouldn't be having it, either, really! But I'm not going to say, 'Oh no, that's just for grown-ups,' because it's not fair—and it makes the sweet thing much more desirable to her."

Carmen, mother of Mila, 2 years

BLW STORY

It took two or three months for me to feel confident about trusting that Benjamin would eat what he needs. You hear people saying, "They've got to have iron after six months . . . they've got to have this, and they've got to have that," and so I used to worry whether he was getting enough goodness. For example, I thought it'd be good for him to have lentils, but I didn't know how to get them into him. I totally forgot that you could put them on toast or rice cakes.

So I panicked a bit and thought: "If I do purées as well as BLW, at least I can be sure that he's getting some nutrition from the foods that he can't easily pick up and chew." I did puréeing for a couple of months, but it took about two hours' work every night just to do all his food for the following day. When he was about ten months he started eating a bit more, and we went back to just doing BLW. I wish I hadn't lost faith, really, because it would have been a lot easier if I'd just kept going.

And, of course, we discovered that Benjamin liked being in control of what he was eating; he far preferred feeding himself to being spoon-fed. He became very suspicious about what was on the spoon. If we managed to get a little bit in, maybe he'd decide to eat it, but, really, we were just shoving a spoon in his mouth to see whether he liked what was on it—and sometimes he did, but sometimes he didn't. It just felt like a big responsibility getting nutrition into him at first.

Jana, mother of Benjamin, 13 months

5 After the Early Days

"It's been fascinating to watch her deal with so many different types of food and see her skills developing. One week she can't manage a handful of rice, and maybe the next week she can, and then you notice that she's able to pick up a few grains of rice between her fingers. And then nothing happens for ages and suddenly she's able to actually pick up a spoon and put it in her own mouth. But we can't teach her anything—we just have to sit back and watch her learn."

Margaret, mother of Esther, 21 months

Progressing at Your Baby's Pace

As your baby progresses with solid food, you'll see her skills develop as she learns to handle a wide range of textures and shapes. However, many parents find that their baby's progress isn't as smooth as they expect. As we've seen, some babies start with enthusiasm, while others seem to take ages to eat very much at all. Expectations about how quickly babies should increase their food intake are often unrealistic and based on a method of weaning in which the parent—not the baby—is in charge. It seems that, when babies are allowed to make their own decisions, very few naturally choose to follow a set pattern. So it's best not to think too much about what "should" happen and just let your baby set the pace.

BLW STORY

They are so different. Ben was interested in eating almost straightaway—I could see from his diapers he was getting some food inside him quite quickly. And it feels as though he wants to eat more than his skills are ready for, so I always have to make sure he has a few bits he can manage easily. He really enjoys squashing stuff into his mouth. He's much messier than Maud was and is nowhere near picking up small things like peas yet. It was so different with her. Mealtimes were like a scientific experiment. She was quite dexterous and could pick up different things quite quickly. She'd lick things and examine them, but she didn't eat much until she was about one. There was hardly any change in her milk feeds until then. But with Ben, he's definitely going for it with food. I'm sure he was taking less at the breast after about three weeks, and I really wasn't expecting that.

Rosie, mother of Maud, 2 years; and Ben, 8 months

If you include your baby in all your own mealtimes and let her decide how many milk feedings she wants, she'll naturally move toward eating whenever you eat (and, later, having as many snacks as she needs) in her own time. But it may not happen as soon as you expect. The old advice that all babies should be on three meals a day by eight months doesn't work with BLW. Although most babies may be keen to handle and play with food three times a day at this age, many still won't be eating much, and, of course, many more won't want anything other than a milk feeding for breakfast. There's no point in trying to rush your baby—it won't make her learn any faster, and she'll probably get upset and frustrated. It's much better to keep mealtimes enjoyable and let her decide when she's ready to eat more.

It's also fairly common for babies to go through a lull at some point between seven and nine months, when progress with solids seems nonexistent. As long as your baby is well, is having plenty of milk feedings, and is included in your mealtimes, this is unlikely to be anything to worry about. Lulls like this are usually short lived and are often followed by a sudden increase in both appetite and feeding skills. Many parents describe this as when their baby suddenly "got it" and started to really eat.

Whether or not you experience a lull, at some point you'll probably notice your baby playing less with her food and eating more purposefully. This can happen any time from eight or nine months to around a year and often (but not always) coincides with the baby gradually asking for less milk; the best approach is to let your baby's appetite and abilities guide you. Keep offering her plenty of opportunities to practice her new skills on a variety of foods, make sure there is someone (you!) for her to copy, and let her take her time. You'll probably find that by around nine or ten months she is eating pretty much the same range of foods as the rest of the family and that you no longer need to think too hard about how to prepare her food because she can manage most things without a problem.

> "When Jake was about a year old, I realized that he was actually starting to eat for eating's sake rather than just getting to know food. There was a definite shift away from play and into eating—as though he needed to fill his belly."
>
> Vicky, mother of Jake, 3 years

Adventurous Taste Buds

Once you and your baby have gotten started with BLW, it's a good idea to make sure she experiences a wide range of flavors. The more variety she has now, the more readily she'll try new things when she's older. Many parents automatically give their baby plain food for the first few weeks of solid foods, but there's no need to restrict your baby to bland flavors. All babies are exposed to different tastes in the womb because they swallow amniotic fluid that contains traces of the flavors of foods the mother has eaten. Breastfed babies get different-tasting milk, too, according to their mother's diet. They usually enjoy new flavors, even quite strong ones, especially if their mother eats them often. In fact, studies suggest that breastfed babies are programmed to accept flavors that are familiar to them from breast milk (for example, garlic), possibly because this is a way of showing them that these foods are safe. And yet many people believe that a baby's first solid foods need to be almost tasteless. In some cultures, there is a belief that young children won't eat vegetables and meat, and as a result they tend to be restricted to cereals, such as rice, until they are as old as two years. This is not only unnecessary but is probably boring for the child, and can lead to undernutrition.

> "We gave Isabella a really wide range of tastes right from the start—as many things as we could think of—and now she'll eat just about anything. It's great when we're traveling. She's always eaten things like sauerkraut, chili, chicken piri piri—she's got broader tastes than many adults I know."
>
> Jennifer, mother of Isabella, 4 years

Using herbs, spices, and strong-flavored vegetables in your cooking is not only good for taste but may be beneficial for the family's health, too, since many of these foods have their own health-giving properties and nutrients. A wide variety of healthy foods and flavors is also more likely to provide your baby with all the essential vitamins and minerals.

Babies who feed themselves are more likely to try unfamiliar foods and to be more adventurous with flavors than babies who are fed by someone else. As we've seen, this may be because food that is under the baby's control can be rejected more easily, whereas food that is puréed is much harder to spit it out if she doesn't like it.

The following tips are useful to bear in mind:

- Always let your baby decide if she wants to eat something—there's no need to persuade her if she doesn't seem to want it.
- Your baby will taste new foods at the front of her mouth and spit them out if she doesn't want them—

it's important not to scold her or try to prevent her from doing this.

- Let your baby copy you at the table—if you are eating something with a strong flavor, such as curry or chili, curiosity will almost certainly make her want to try it.
- Give your baby the chance to try foods that you don't normally eat, so she is offered the maximum variety of tastes.

Some parents of babies who have had only formula (and whose feedings for the first six months have therefore all tasted the same) have noticed that their babies are less adventurous with flavors at first. This doesn't usually last long, though; most are keen to experiment, even with strong flavors.

Many BLW babies have surprised their parents by tasting some spicy or hot food and then going back for more. Even if there are foods that you only have now and then, or when you eat out, try to include your baby in the meal so she can taste it, too. (As long as it's not *too* hot, of course—don't expect her to enjoy the hottest chiles just yet!) Most spicy dishes are served with something plain, such as rice or noodles, so there'll be something else she can eat if she wants to. Have some water or plain yogurt on hand in case she does find the food too spicy—and remember to taste the food yourself first and take out any hot chile peppers before your baby tries it.

However hesitant your baby is, the more opportunities she is given to try different foods and the more she is able to copy the example of others, the less cautious she is likely to be as time goes on. There's no need to coax her if there's something she doesn't want to taste; some foods have very strong smells that she may need to get used to.

> **"When Harriet was about nine months old, we went out for a curry. She was eating rice really well by then and she grabbed a handful from my plate, and it had some curry sauce on it. The thing is, the curry was really hot—it was actually too hot for me. Before I could do anything, she had crammed it into her mouth. I was expecting her to go completely ballistic. But she just sort of thought about it, then swallowed it and reached for some more."** Jen, mother of Harriet, 2 years

Introducing spicy foods

Most cultures that have a lot of spicy foods start babies off with mild versions of the family dishes. A simple, thick stew made from lentils can be a good way to do this. You can add all sorts of vegetables and gradually increase the amounts of spices or try different combinations. Lentils are nutritious, with lots of protein and iron. Pita, tortilla, or toast can be used as a dipper, or the dal can be eaten in handfuls or in balls mixed with rice or offered to your baby on a preloaded spoon so she can feed herself with it.

Learning About Textures

As well as offering your baby a variety of flavors, remember that she also needs to experience different textures. If you eat a varied diet, most textures—runny, crunchy, chewy, mushy, and so on—are likely to be in your meals anyway, so there's no need to limit your baby to foods you think she'll be able to manage easily. Exploring a full range of textures will help her to develop important skills that are relevant to eating, the prevention of choking, oral hygiene, and possibly even speech. She'll also enjoy discovering different consistencies.

Your baby will probably be remarkably inventive at getting foods of different textures into her mouth before she learns to use cutlery—even if she does get covered in whatever it is she is trying to eat. She may suck at spaghetti, shovel rice or ground meat into her mouth, gnaw at chicken bones, try eating straight off the plate, lick the plate clean, or pick up peas one by one. Whatever food is being offered, your baby will find a way to tackle it.

Textures don't only come in hard and soft—there are lots of in-betweens and subtle differences. For example:

- Roasted vegetables have a crunchy outside but a soft inside, while other vegetables can be either crisp or mushy, depending on how long you cook them.
- Toasted bread crusts are hard and dry, whereas cucumber is firm but moist.
- Pears can be hard or soft (and really juicy!), depending on how ripe they are.
- Foods such as wafer cookies are crunchy to bite but go soft almost as soon as they hit the tongue.
- Bananas are firm to bite, then soft to chew, while mashed potato is soft to bite *and* chew.
- Cheddar cheese is hard and can be sucked for ages, Edam cheese is rubbery, and feta cheese crumbles easily.

- Meat is springy, while white fish is often soft and crumbly.
- Mashed potato can be dry and floury, soft and sticky, or almost runny.
- A chicken drumstick has both the texture of the flesh and the hardness of the bone (and working out how to separate the meat from the bone can be challenging and fun).
- Nut butters and soft cheeses are sticky (so they'll need to be spread thinly at first until your baby discovers how to use her tongue to help her move them around her mouth).

Crunchy textures are fun

Research suggests that we get particular enjoyment out of eating crunchy foods. It seems that massive bursts of ultrasound are generated with the very first bite and that these trigger pleasure receptors in the brain. This suggests that babies who are given only purées at first are missing out on an important source of pleasure—something that BLW babies may associate with mealtimes for years to come.

"Naresh first took some rice from my plate when he was about eight and a half months—a handful at first, and then he started picking it up grain by grain and very carefully putting each grain into his mouth. It hadn't occurred to me to offer him anything other than sticks of vegetables until then. It always takes me by surprise how well he can manage different foods."

Rashmi, mother of Naresh, 10 months

Although most parents enjoy seeing how inventive their baby is with different textures, they often draw the line at letting their baby feed herself with runny food, perhaps dreading the inevitable mess. Most semiliquid foods can be adapted (see pages 136–38) to make them easier for babies to manage, and it's important for babies to experience all sorts of textures—not just the ones that are less messy.

The key to success with BLW is to see things from the baby's point of view and to try to forget the rules that adults apply to eating. If the rest of the family is eating runny food, offer some to your baby and try not to worry about her table manners for now; they'll come eventually. She needs to master food in her own way first. As for the mess, well, there's nothing you can do to prevent it, but you can prepare for it so it's not too much work to clean up (see pages 100–03). Remember that you don't have to give your child runny food every day and that this stage of messy eating doesn't last long. You'll miss the cute baby face covered in yogurt when she's older—honestly!

It's not uncommon for babies to develop phobias, as toddlers, over foods that they associate with an unpleasant atmosphere, and it's easy to see how runny or messy food could be a problem later if a baby's early experiences with them are stressful. So don't scold your baby for making a mess or let her know that it bothers you; always keep mealtimes enjoyable.

Feast and Famine

Once your baby has been sharing your mealtimes for a few months, you can expect to see a pattern emerging with her food intake as she learns that food can keep her from feeling hungry. You may be surprised at just how much the amount she eats varies—from feast one day to famine the next. Some babies go days without apparently eating much at all, then suddenly switch to eating everything in sight. As long as you offer her nutritious food, you simply need to trust your baby's appetite and instinct to know what she needs and when she needs it. If she is still asking for plenty of milk feedings, she is not going to go hungry.

Sometimes a baby will lose interest in solid food for a few days for a particular reason, for example:

- Teething: It may hurt the baby to eat solid food, and she may need the comfort of breast or bottle instead (breastfeeding is especially good for easing teething pain).
- A cold or other minor infection: Digesting food takes considerable energy, and not eating gives the baby a chance to use all her energy to fight the infection. Once the cold has gone, everything should go back to normal.
- Other illnesses: Loss of appetite with other signs, such as paleness, listlessness, or persistent crying, suggests the baby is ill and should be checked by a doctor.
- Emotional issues: Changes such as the arrival of a new sibling; parents going back to work; a new nursery, nanny, or caretaker; moving houses; and going on vacation can all affect a baby's appetite temporarily.

It's important not to try to persuade your baby to eat by coaxing or forcing her. This will probably only make her confused and upset and could also risk creating an unhappy attitude to food. Bear in mind that no baby or young child will starve herself intentionally; provided nourishing food is available, babies will always eat according to their needs, and if they miss a few days, they'll make up for it when they need to.

> **"I would probably describe Robert as a typical child when it comes to eating: He'll eat nothing for three days, and then he'll eat lots for the next three days. I was exactly the same—apparently my mom would always say, 'I'm not worried, because I know that in a few days, she'll eat like a horse.'"**
>
> Kath, mother of Euan, 3 years; and Robert, 18 months

Eating Enough: Learning to Trust Your Baby

One of the hardest parts of BLW for many parents is trusting their baby to eat as much as she needs. The amounts BLW babies eat can continue to seem very small, even when they are beginning to eat purposefully (as opposed to just exploring), and it can be difficult to believe that they know what they are doing.

Parents who have been formula-feeding may be used to having a fair amount of control over their baby's feedings and are generally guided on how much to give by the recommendations of the formula manufacturer or by health professionals. Also, formula-fed babies tend to have roughly the same amount of milk at each feeding. So if you are used to formula-feeding, it may take you a while to feel confident trusting your baby to know how much and how often she needs to eat.

Parents who have been used to breastfeeding can also find it hard to believe their baby is eating the "right" amount even though they have already learned to trust her to eat and drink as much as she needs. Your baby is the expert on her own unique appetite and needs. If you are worried that she is not eating enough, it may help to remember the following:

- Our ideas about how much babies should eat tend to be based on the old belief that a chubby baby was a healthy baby.
- Puréed food is often mixed with water or milk, which makes it look like much more than it really is—with BLW, it's all food.
- Babies of the same age, weight, and activity level may need to eat very different amounts because their metabolisms are different (we all know healthy adults who seem to live on thin air).
- Babies have small tummies (about the size of their fist); they need to eat little and often. They can't usually eat large amounts at every meal.
- The first solid foods are supposed to complement the baby's milk diet, not replace it. Breast milk or formula is still a baby's main source of nutrition in the early months of solids and remains the most important part of their diet until they are at least a year old.

> **"When we talk about mealtimes, my parents will say, 'Did you manage to get any food into Keira?' But it's not about getting food into her. Keira's quite capable of feeding herself, so she's not going to starve; if she's hungry, and there's food, then she'll eat."**
>
> Jennie, mother of Keira, 2 years

Sometimes it comes down to tricking yourself into feeling good about what your baby has eaten. If you give her a small amount of food and she wants more, you'll be pleased. If you give her a large plateful and she can't manage it all, you may be disappointed. But the chances are she will eat exactly the same amount—as much as she needs—whichever way you do it!

In general, if your baby is filling and wetting her diapers normally and is healthy and thriving, then you can be confident that she is eating enough.

BLW STORY

When Mia got to three or four months, her grandparents were all saying that she should be eating solids. But Mia just wasn't interested—I really felt under pressure. I tried offering food at six months, but she'd just play with it—she wasn't even putting anything in her mouth at that age. I remember going out with some friends from my prenatal group and all the other babies were being spoon-fed a main course, a dessert, then maybe a little cookie to finish. And Mia wasn't eating anything—I was just breastfeeding. So, of course, I started to wonder if she was ever going to eat.

I wasn't very confident at that stage. I was worried that she was just playing and not really eating, but I just kept offering her something at every mealtime and she gradually started eating. But even then 90 percent of it ended up on the floor; I don't think she got much inside her till about eight months. It took me quite a while to trust that she really could feed herself. I needed the confidence to know that if she's happy and growing and she has the opportunity to eat, then she's obviously not starving.

I just don't worry about it anymore. Some days she'll eat loads, and then she might not eat anything much for a couple of days. But she really enjoys food now. She eats things that most babies probably don't even have the chance to try—like olives and chorizo and spicy foods. It's really good she's got such a broad palate already. Most people seem quite surprised. My Italian parents-in-law were very doubtful about the way we introduced her to solids—until we went around there for a meal and, at eleven months, Mia ate a whole bowlful of pasta.

Joanna, mother of Mia, 17 months

Telling You She's Had Enough

A baby who can't yet talk isn't able to tell her parents, "I've had enough, thanks," but babies can signal that they don't want any more of a particular food, or that the meal is over, especially when they have been doing BLW for a few months. They may pick up individual pieces of food and drop them one by one over the edge of their high chair, or they may sweep everything off their tray. Some babies are more subtle: They simply start shaking their heads or handing pieces of food to their parents. Some parents teach their babies sign language to help them communicate their needs. Either way, the message usually becomes clear.

In the early weeks of BLW, it can be more difficult to tell when a baby is signaling that she has had enough, because throwing and dropping food are less purposeful. Luckily, at this stage a meal is not really about eating; it's for learning about tastes and exploring food, so there's no need to be concerned that your baby won't have eaten what she needs.

The key to ensuring that your baby has enough to eat is always to offer more—perhaps something different or something from your plate (even if it's the same as the food she has)—without any expectation that she will eat it. That way she can turn it down if she doesn't need it without you feeling disappointed. This is much safer than assuming that she's had enough just because her plate (or tray) is empty. But don't keep doing it for too long: Continuing to give your baby back pieces of food that she is trying to tell you she doesn't want is likely to make her frustrated and angry, because she's not managing to make you understand.

> **"Finn went through a phase of telling us he had had enough by clearing the tray himself, with his whole arm and hand extended like a windshield wiper! It was very effective and a clear signal he was done with that course. Since we have given him a plate or bowl, he does the windshield-wipering less, and instead I ask him to place the bits on the plate. This often works as a distraction—but sometimes if he's fed up the whole plate will go!"**
>
> Mae'r, mother of Finn, 11 months

BLW STORY

I really enjoy watching Madeleine choosing what she's going to pick up; it's such a definite action when they pick it up themselves. We spoon-fed our first child, Noah, and I remember finding the mush stage really boring. After a while, offering the spoon and getting the shut mouth reply gets very tedious; I remember thinking that I'd rather do three diaper changes than one mealtime.

It's completely different with Madeleine. Because she's picking things up herself quite happily, you can see when she's hungry—she's chewing everything quite quickly and getting it down. And then you can see her gradually slow down, until she starts playing with it and dropping it over the side of the high chair. It's the clear indication that "this meal's over, I've had enough."

Nick, father of Noah, 4 years; and Madeleine, 8 months

Food Fads

Closely linked to worries about *how much* young children eat are concerns about *what* they eat. Older babies and toddlers often go through phases of what may seem like "picky" eating when all they want is one particular food for days at a time. Although it can be baffling if your BLW baby suddenly wants to eat nothing but bananas, fads like this seem to be natural behavior; they shouldn't be confused with the fussiness seen in children who are using food as part of a battle of wills with their parents.

Babies and small children seem to know instinctively which foods will give them the nutrients they need. Many parents have noticed that food fads coincide with their baby's general development or health; for example, babies and toddlers often seem to focus on protein or carbohydrates during periods of rapid growth or intense activity, and on foods such as fruit or on breast milk when recovering from an illness. Some appear to be able to identify foods to which they are allergic or intolerant. If it really is babies' survival instinct that drives them to behave like this, it's no wonder they react so strongly when they are forced to eat something they don't want!

It seems that it's natural for babies to want to eat a single food (or a small group of foods) for several days—and then, quite suddenly, to not want to eat those foods at all. It's unlikely they will become undernourished, since most foods contain several nutrients (not just one type) and very few need to be eaten every day.

Baby-led weaning babies also show their preferences—and possibly their need—for certain foods by choosing what to eat first at each meal. Some parents have noticed that their children make a beeline for foods that are rich in fat when the weather is cold (fat is a concentrated source of calories, which are used up faster when the body needs to keep warm). Other babies go for meat or dark green vegetables first—possibly when they need some extra iron.

"I always felt I could tell when the weather was turning colder when I found my children's fingermarks in the butter."

Mary, mother of two and grandmother of three

> "I remember when Charlotte was ill with some sort of virus and all she ate was protein. It was bizarre. And on another occasion, we went on vacation when she was about two and a half, and all she ate was carbohydrates, and she grew about three centimeters in a couple of weeks. It was fascinating. I am a great believer that they will take what they need to suit their requirements."
>
> Barbara, mother of Charlotte, 6 years; and David, 2 years

If babies are responding to a need when they crave a particular food, it's important to trust their instinct and let them make these choices. Allowing children to make decisions about food doesn't encourage them to become fussy; it's generally children who feel they have no control over their eating who are more likely to limit the foods they'll eat later in life.

Food fads are unpredictable, so don't assume that, just because your baby wanted nothing but mango yesterday, there's no point in offering her other foods today. Babies who are too young to talk can't ask for the foods they need; instead they show us what they want by choosing some foods—and turning down others—from the selection they are offered.

Just as your baby may binge on certain foods, she may "go off" a particular food, too—even one she previously liked. It's best to accept that this food may be rejected for quite a while, but there's no need to worry about whether or not to include it in future meals; if it's on the family menu, just keep offering it (without pushing it). If she sees you eating it and has the chance to try it again, there's every chance your baby will change her mind. But if you don't offer it, you won't know when she's ready to give it another try.

If your child goes through food fads, try to be relaxed about how extreme they seem to be and how long they last. This is easier said than done, but, if you are finding yourself getting wound up about your baby's apparent refusal to eat anything except blueberries, ask yourself what the alternative is. Most mealtime battles don't start with a child refusing to eat but with a parent insisting that she does! Very few of these battles are won by the parents, and then only at the expense of a happy parent-child relationship. In other words, going to war with your child is not the answer. If they're allowed to run their course, food fads don't tend to last more than a few weeks at most.

> **"Jacob went through a banana phase, when he would just eat a whole banana for breakfast every morning for about two weeks. And then of course one day, that was it, he didn't want banana anymore. He'll have a little bit, but not like he used to."**
>
> Steve, father of Jacob, 8 months

Your Baby's Appetite for Milk Feedings

Babies grow more in their first year than at any other time in their lives, and they need nutrient- and calorie-rich breast milk or formula to do this; solid foods—whatever they are—don't contain anywhere near as much concentrated nourishment. So don't be surprised if your baby shows no signs of wanting to replace her milk feedings for several months after taking her first mouthful of food.

As we've seen, when babies first start eating solid foods, all they are really doing is discovering different tastes and textures and allowing their bodies to adjust gradually to digesting new foods. As they begin to eat more at mealtimes, the need for breast milk or formula diminishes; how fast this happens varies enormously from baby to baby.

How you and your baby experience the gradual cutting down of milk feedings will also differ depending on whether you are breastfeeding or formula-feeding. If you are breastfeeding and letting her have all her drinks at the breast, you may not notice any change in the number of feedings she has each day, though they may get shorter. If you are formula-feeding, you can expect her to be having only one or two milk feedings a day by the time she is a year old. If you have been combining breastfeeding with formula-feeding, you will probably find that you can cut out the formula feedings and keep the breastfeeding going. Doing it this way will ensure that you and your child benefit for longer from the health advantages that come with breastfeeding.

Whether you are breastfeeding, formula-feeding, or doing a combination of the two, it's best, at first, to think of milk feedings and mealtimes as two different things. In the early days, if your baby is hungry, she wants (and needs) milk. She has no idea that other foods can fill her up and won't enjoy being put in a high chair and given pieces of food to play with when what she really wants is her milk. Thinking of milk feedings as separate from mealtimes will also mean that reducing milk feedings will happen naturally, as your baby's need for them lessens.

As your baby begins to eat more at each mealtime, she will either ask for her next milk feeding slightly later than usual or she will take less milk at that feeding. When she is eating more substantial amounts and having a drink of water (or a short breastfeed) with her meals, she will simply begin to miss out some of her main milk feedings. As long as you listen to what she is "telling" you (if she wants milk, she'll ask for a feeding in her usual way; if she doesn't, she'll turn away when offered the breast or bottle) and don't try to make her take more or less milk than she wants, you'll be able to rely on her appetite to let you know what to do.

> **"Luke's probably dropped one feed—if not two—already. But when he first started solids, he would often want milk afterward, and I remember saying: 'He wants more milk now than he did before.' But I think that was a phase after the new food. Breastfeeding is so dependent on other things—whether he's tired, or teething, or feeling poorly. If he's tired, he'll quite often have some dinner and go straight on the boob afterward."**
>
> Anna, mother of Luke, 8 months

The way your baby cuts down her milk feedings can also work in reverse, so it's very flexible. There may be days when she is less interested in solid foods or when, for whatever reason, you aren't able to offer her as many meals as usual. Or it may be that she's not feeling well or is teething and wants the comfort of milk feeding. On those days, her appetite for milk will probably increase, so that she doesn't go hungry. If you are formula-feeding, you will simply need to let her have more formula; if you are breastfeeding, allowing her to feed as often as she wants will stimulate your body to make more milk—even if your supply had already begun to go down.

> "I didn't notice much change in the breastfeeding. The food was just on top of the breast milk, and Austin seemed to increase the amount of calories he was getting from food very, very gradually. He's a big boy, Austin. I don't know if that's got anything to do with it."
>
> Bryony, mother of Austin, 22 months

> "When we started, we just kept going with the same amount of formula. It didn't seem to change for ages, and we seemed to be doing nothing but feeding, with either formula or solids. Then when Chloe was about nine months, she just forgot to ask for her afternoon bottle one day—so I didn't remind her. She didn't seem to miss that bottle and didn't go back to it. I was really surprised—I thought I'd have to decide more for her because I was bottle-feeding."
>
> Helen, mother of Chloe, 15 months

Three Meals a Day?

Once your baby decides to cut down on milk feedings, she may also be hungry between meals. Human babies are natural "grazers." That is, they naturally eat little and often. It's only as we get older that we train ourselves to eat large meals infrequently (though whether this is a good thing is open to debate). Babies' stomachs are far too small to be limited to three meals a day, especially once they are having fewer milk feedings. Most babies simply don't have the capacity to eat enough to keep them going for four or five hours during the day without food.

So once your baby has really gotten going with solids and is asking for fewer or smaller milk feedings, you can start to offer her healthy snacks. Allowing her to eat good food, little and often, also has the advantage of making you less likely to worry when the amount she eats at "official" mealtimes is small. Remember, though, that it's only by offering that you can find out what your baby wants; don't push her to have a snack if she wants a milk feeding.

For a baby under about eighteen months, there is no need to make a distinction between snacks and meals, either in relation to where and when they happen or in terms of how big they are. They just need to be nutritious and, between them, give your baby the chance to eat something from all the main food groups each day (see pages 193–95). Young children should continue to be offered food (either as snacks or meals) about six or more times a day, for several years. Offering frequent nutritious snacks is also one of the best ways to prevent young children from asking for sweets and junk food. But remember that, as with her meals, if your baby turns down an offered snack, she is simply telling you she doesn't need it.

Many foods marketed as snacks are not healthy. Often adults and older children reach for foods such as chips, chocolate bars, and sodas when they feel a little hungry or thirsty, but these foods are not good for anyone: babies, children, or adults. They are usually heavy in salt and/or sugar, as well as additives, and provide a short-term energy rush with very little actual nourishment. Sugary foods are bad for teeth at all ages, even before baby teeth have come in.

Since many highly processed snack foods lack any real nutritional value, they should be given only if your child is hungry and absolutely nothing else is available. Taking snack foods such as a banana or plain rice cake with you whenever you are out should make these occasions rare (see page 142 for ideas for snacks). If you do need to let your baby have foods that have little nutritional value, try to keep the amount to a minimum so that she isn't so full that she can't manage her next meal.

Safe snacking

Snacks should be treated exactly the same way as mealtimes in terms of safety. Make sure your baby is sitting up (supported if necessary) when she is eating or handling food and that an adult is with her at all times. Eating while being pushed in a stroller should be avoided in case your baby is jolted as she eats. She shouldn't eat snacks (or meals) while she is distracted, for example, when watching TV.

Many of the foods that you will be offering your baby at mealtimes can work just as well as a snack, and thinking of all your baby's snacks as mini-meals will help you choose nutritious foods to give her, whatever the time of day. Nutritious snacks add to your baby's well-being—it's only nonnutritious ones that are a problem.

Your Baby's Diaper

One of the biggest changes you'll notice soon after your baby starts on solids is the change in her poop. The poop of a fully breastfed baby is soft, runny, and yellow and smells very mild (almost sweet, some parents say). For the first month or so of life, breastfed babies poop several times a day, but after four to six weeks they can change to pooping only once every few days. Some have been known to go as long as three weeks without pooping. Provided the baby is otherwise well, long gaps between poops is perfectly normal; it is not constipation.

Formula-fed babies have a slightly darker and more formed stool from birth, and their poop smells slightly stronger than breastfed babies' poop. They can also become constipated, which is why parents are often advised to offer them extra drinks of water, especially in hot weather.

Straining to poop

Some babies appear to strain to pass a poop, even when the poop itself is quite soft. It's not clear why this is, but it doesn't seem to be related to what or how they eat. One theory says that straining starts to happen when the baby discovers that she can actually control this process—and that she may even get some enjoyment out of it!

With BLW, the first sign that your baby has actually swallowed some food may well be when you see "bits" in her poop (this tends to be more obvious in the soft poop of a breastfed baby). You may even be able to recognize the food from earlier that day or the day before (sometimes this is not at all what you'd expect: for example, banana can appear as black wormlike streaks!). This doesn't mean that your baby can't digest the food; it just shows that her body is adjusting to it and developing the enzymes needed to break it down. The bits will be less recognizable as she learns to chew foods thoroughly before swallowing.

Gradually, your baby's poop will become slightly more solid and darker in color. It shouldn't be really hard, though. Persistently hard or unusually runny poop, especially if accompanied by other signs of illness such as vomiting or a raised temperature, should always be checked by a doctor.

The most noticeable change in your baby's poop as she starts to eat solid foods will be the smell! This can be quite unexpected when you have gotten used to the smell of poop from a milk-only diet, but it is perfectly normal. Your baby may pass wind slightly more often, too—or it may just be that her farts are more noticeable because they are smelly!

Some babies get a slightly sore bottom when their poop starts to change. If this happens, you just need to be alert and ready to change your baby's diaper the minute she has filled it.

"His poop changed quite soon; it was only about five or six weeks in. We were so proud—it was Cameron's first proper poop. He was only pooping a couple of times a week before; now it's every day. And it's never changed back—he must be eating more than we realize."

Sophie, mother of Cameron, 8 months

"Alanna started putting food in her mouth from around six and a half months, but her poop didn't seem to change for ages. Up until nine or ten months, everything seemed to come out as it went in—we'd just see little bits of carrot or red peppers in an otherwise liquidy, breastfed poop. When she started to really dig into her food, her poop gradually became much more solid."

Monica, mother of Alanna, 15 months

Experimenting with food and drink

Your baby might enjoy exploring what can be put into a cup as well as what comes out of it. She may be fascinated to discover which foods float and which ones sink. While adults may not like their drinks to taste of Brussels sprouts or fish, this is unlikely to worry your baby. It's a good idea, though, to take out any small pieces of food from her cup before she drinks, to minimize the risk of choking.

Introducing a Cup

Your baby will probably be curious about drinking from a cup as soon as she starts sharing meals with you. Even though she won't yet recognize it as a way to quench her thirst, it's a good idea to start offering her some water with her food.

Although training or "sippy" cups with a spout can be very useful when you are out and about because they reduce the risk of spills, letting your baby practice with a real cup when you're at home will help her to learn faster. It will also be better for her teeth and for the development of her mouth.

Babies need to work out how to tip a cup up just enough to be able to drink, but not so much that they get wet. Slanted cups are designed to help babies learn about tipping; they need to be tipped less than standard cups, and the baby has a clearer view of what's in the cup and what happens when it's tipped. However, they are not necessarily easier to manage than a standard open cup; see what works for your baby.

The most important thing to consider is the width of the cup; choose one that is smaller than you would use yourself (about the size of a shot glass or an espresso cup). Offering your baby a wide-rimmed cup (whether straight or slanted) is like asking an adult to drink from a bucket; most of the liquid will go down the sides of the baby's chin.

Babies often find a full cup easier to manage than a half-full one, because it doesn't need to be tipped up as far. If you choose a small cup, which needs only a small amount of water to fill it, there will be less to mop up if it spills!

Babies learn by exploring and experimenting. They can't be expected to know what happens when a cup is tipped up if they haven't been allowed to try. And they don't know that pouring water over the table matters. Allowing your baby to practice pouring games at the sink or in the bath can help her learn how a cup works and may mean she needs to experiment less at the table.

Introducing Cutlery

Once your child has become a skilled self-feeder, you may start to wonder if she'll ever learn to use cutlery. But there's no need to worry; she won't always eat with her fingers. Small children have a strong drive to copy those around them, so unless you always eat with your hands, the chances are she'll want to experiment with a knife and fork. Once she's mastered the basics of eating, set a place for her with her own cutlery. Choose a child-sized set: Asking a baby to use adult-sized cutlery is the equivalent of expecting an adult to eat with salad servers!

As with food, it's best not to expect too much of your baby too soon. To start with, she will see cutlery as part of playing and copying, not as a way to get food into her mouth. For that, her fingers will be a lot more efficient. Eventually, in her own time, she'll work out what to do with a fork or spoon (using a knife will take quite a bit longer). Trying to encourage, force, or teach her to use cutlery before she is ready will only upset and frustrate her.

Some babies attempt to use cutlery only occasionally for many months because they know they'll get more food if they use their hands; others get the hang of it very quickly. Most babies, though, are beginning to use a spoon or fork by their first birthday. As long as you let your baby have plenty of practice with different textures and shapes, she will learn to manage cutlery efficiently, at her own pace.

Although most parents give their baby a spoon to start with, many babies find a fork easier in the beginning. Spoons work best in a bowl, with sloppy food—as you know from feeding yourself. Getting food onto a spoon from a flat plate can be difficult, and keeping it on the spoon while you get it to your mouth is quite tricky, too. Forks are much easier to load than spoons because spearing a piece of food is usually easier than scooping it up, and the food tends to stay on a fork even if it's turned upside down. So you may want to go for a fork, initially, rather than a spoon. The fork you choose doesn't have to be one designed for a baby, but it should be small enough for her to manage. Make sure that the prongs are not so thick that they crush the food rather than spearing it, nor so thin or pointed that they could cause an injury.

Working out how to use a "dipper" (such as a cooked green bean or breadstick; see pages 137–38) can be useful preparation for learning how to use a spoon, so you might want to start with that first. You could also try handing your baby a ready-loaded spoon or letting her guide your hand while you hold it, as this will also help her understand how a spoon works; babies can take food off a spoon with their mouths before they are able to load one themselves. Don't be surprised if, the first few times, she turns the spoon upside down and loses everything on it—or flings the food across the room when she waves her arm. She doesn't know this is going to happen until she's done it a few times—and even then it will be a long time before she understands that it actually *matters* if food is thrown around! So expect some mess—or, if the weather is good, let her early experiments with spoons happen outside!

> "Oliver always had a teaspoon at mealtimes, even before he started eating, just so he could join in. At about eleven months, I bought him his own set of cutlery, and he just copied us. At first, I would put some oatmeal onto a spoon and then hand it to him. He was quite good at getting it to his mouth, because he could see me eating my oatmeal at the same time. And he'd use his hands, too, which was fine. Now, though, he wants to use the big cutlery."
>
> Carmel, mother of Oliver, 14 months

When your child does start to use cutlery (rather than just play with it), she'll be very slow. So take a deep breath and be patient. It can be agonizing to watch a young child attempt, time after time, to get a piece of food onto her fork or spoon, only to see it fall off on the way to her mouth. Your baby will do this many, many times before she masters using cutlery. Try not to interfere or help her too much—however hard it seems to be for her—she'll learn faster if she is allowed to work it out for herself. Your baby's personality will dictate how quickly she gets frustrated and goes back to using her fingers for the rest of the meal, but, if she's the patient, tenacious type, be prepared for meals to take some time.

"Mason will spend absolutely ages working very hard to use his cutlery. He uses the fork to try to stab the food, and often, rather than eating it himself, he will offer it to me. He occasionally manages to get it into his own mouth as well, but he's still really learning to do it. So our mealtimes have become a bit more leisurely recently. He goes back to his hands sometimes, but he's surprisingly persistent with his cutlery."

Jo, mother of Mason, 16 months

Tips for helping your baby use cutlery

- Forks are easier for most babies to use than spoons at first.
- Dippers and ready-loaded spoons can help your baby learn how a spoon works.
- Have a spoon and fork within your baby's reach so she can experiment with them when she's ready.
- Be patient—her progress will be quite slow.
- Don't try to help unless she asks you to.

"Rosie's a neat little eater now, even though it was so messy to start with. She sits very nicely and really understands that meals are sociable settings."

Stacey, mother of Grace, 4 years;
and Rosie, 14 months

Eating Out

Eating out as a family is one of the great joys of BLW. In the early months, you don't have to worry about taking along preprepared purées and asking busy waiters to provide bowls of hot water or search for a microwave to heat them up—and you don't have to watch your food get cold while you feed your baby. Most restaurants will have something on the menu that she can eat, although at first it will probably be easier just to share your own meal with her.

Many cafés and restaurants will provide a child's portion (or a starter-size portion) of an adult dish if you ask them. Lots of dishes are suitable—from baked potato with tuna to the most elaborate restaurant food—especially once your baby's past the first few months of solids. You'll soon get a feel for what she can manage.

Ordering a range of starter-size portions of main dishes for all of you to share can be great fun for your baby, giving her the opportunity to try lots of new tastes. Turkish meze (pita bread, hummus, marinated peppers, etc.) and Spanish tapas can usually be eaten easily with fingers and are good for sharing. Allowing your baby to choose from what everyone else is eating can be easier than trying to decide on a separate dish for her.

"A friend and I went for lunch with our babies when they were about 10 months old. We ordered lots of starters that we could all share and that they could eat easily with their hands and we just put it on the table. It was brilliant; we were chatting and the two babies were grabbing bits of food and entertaining themselves. We were completely relaxed."

Chantelle, mother of Abby, 2 years

Kids' menus in restaurants

One of the advantages of BLW is that there is no need to turn to the kids' menu in restaurants or limit your choice of where to eat to places serving "child-friendly" food. Your child will be used to normal, nutritious family food, so you won't have to resort to processed chicken nuggets and fries because "that's all she'll eat." Most so-called kids' food is high in salt, sugar, and additives, all of which are bad for children; the longer you can protect your child from junk food, the better.

While children's menus seem to be in almost every restaurant in the US, they're unknown in many other countries, where children simply eat smaller portions of the same food as their parents.

Thinking ahead

Not all restaurants clean their high chairs thoroughly, so you may want to take along some antibacterial wipes to use on the chair before you put your baby into it—especially if she has not yet mastered eating off a plate. Be aware that it's not just the tray you need to clean—the child who used the chair last will probably have smeared his dinner in all the places your child finds to put hers! Some parents take along their baby's own roll-up place mat so that they can be confident she is eating off a clean surface.

> **"When mine were little, I always carried baby wipes with me wherever we went. You never know when you'll need them, whether it's wiping sticky fingers, grubby tables, or dirty bottoms. Even now, if something spills, my children always expect me to have a baby wipe on me."**
>
> Diana, mother of Abigail, 14 years; and Bethany, 12 years

If you eat out a lot, it may be a good idea to buy a clamp-on seat that can be attached to most types of tables. These are useful if a restaurant has a limited number of high chairs and means your baby will sit up at the table with everyone else, so she feels included.

Deciding what to offer your baby to eat in a restaurant or café is fairly easy, but meals usually last much longer than they do at home, and there can be long gaps between courses. Babies and toddlers are naturally curious about their surroundings; your baby will probably find this new environment fascinating and want to explore. She can't be expected to sit still for long periods with nothing to do before the meal arrives or after she's finished eating. After all, you don't normally keep her waiting twenty minutes for her food without allowing her to play, and she's too young to understand that eating out has different rules from eating at home. Be prepared to take her for a walk around the restaurant or outside, or distract her with some toys to keep her from getting bored.

Thinking ahead and seeing eating out from your child's point of view will help to make the outing enjoyable for everyone.

Tips for keeping meals out stress-free

- Order your baby's meal as soon as you can—if it comes with the starters, she'll probably still be happily eating it when the main dishes arrive. Let her eat at her own pace, regardless of which course everyone else is eating.
- Delay sitting your baby in her seat until the meal is about to arrive (or has arrived and cooled down).
- Take along some small toys to keep her occupied at the table.
- Check that the food and the plate aren't too hot—it's a good idea to ask the waiter to put your baby's plate in the middle of the table rather than in front of her, so you can check it before she grabs anything.
- Let your baby feed herself—and resist the temptation to coax her to eat more than she wants, or taste something she doesn't want to, no matter how much you're paying for it.
- Take along her own cup, so you don't have to worry about how she will manage a big restaurant glass.
- If your baby likes to use (or play with) cutlery, take her own set with you.
- If you are worried about the mess, take along your own splash mat so you can pick up the bits from the floor easily once your baby has finished eating.

"Caroline was always a very sociable eater; she would quite happily come to a restaurant with us and sit and eat whatever it was we were eating. I remember her eating monkfish and prawns, just after she was a year old. The whole experience of sharing a meal seemed quite important for her."

Bethany, mother of Caroline, 6 years;
and Daniel, 2 years

"We really enjoy going out for meals, and Brendan eats well in restaurants. We try to order very quickly, and then one of us will usually just go for a walk with him, either around the restaurant or outside the restaurant along the street; we try not to sit him in the high chair until the food arrives. He's not very easily entertained with toys in restaurants, but he will usually sit very nicely as soon as the food is in front of him."

Maxine, mother of Brendan, 17 months

Picnics

Baby-led weaning works particularly well for picnics. Most picnic food is designed to be eaten with fingers, which is exactly what your baby is used to doing. There are no concerns about mess, and there's usually no hurry, so it can be even easier to share a picnic than a meal around the table.

You don't have to go far to have a picnic—your backyard or the local park are fine—and if the weather is bad, you could even have one on a mat indoors!

BLW and Childcare

Most daycare staff, nannies, and grandparents are very open to BLW, especially once they see it in action. It's common for grandparents, especially, to be doubtful at the outset and then, after seeing their grandchildren feed themselves, say that they regret not knowing about BLW when their own children were babies.

However, if the person who will be caring for your baby has spent years introducing babies to solids using spoon-feeding, they may not understand why you aren't happy for them to feed your baby this way when she is with them. It may help to remind them that they would have encouraged their babies to start finger foods from about six months, so all you are doing (and asking them to do) is to skip the purée stage.

> **"People have a picture in their mind of a baby starting solids, and for a lot of people, that picture is of a lying-back sixteen-week-old baby. But when you explain that you're not talking about that baby, you're talking about an older baby who can sit up and pick things up and chew, it begins to make sense to them."**
>
> Katie, mother of Sammy, 5 years; and Elvis, 2 years

If your baby's caretaker is not experienced with BLW, you'll need to see things from their point of view so you can anticipate any likely challenges. One of the common stumbling blocks is expectations about how much a baby will eat. Most grandparents and nannies would feel they were neglecting a basic duty if a child didn't eat "enough." If you are leaving your baby in someone else's care at the very beginning of BLW, it's important to make sure they understand that, at this stage, mealtimes are for learning and playing, and that it's OK if your baby doesn't eat any solid food in the first few weeks. The idea that they shouldn't offer your baby food when she is hungry for a milk feeding may feel strange to them, too, so they need to know why this is important (see page 79).

Older babies sometimes become less adventurous with food for the first few weeks after a change of caretaker, just until they get used to the new situation. Your baby may want only familiar foods for a few days, or even lose her appetite for anything but milk feedings. Make sure her caretaker knows that as long as your baby is offered a variety of foods, it doesn't matter how much or how little she eats.

> "Sometimes Amy's day care provider would give her things chopped up too small, and Amy couldn't pick them up. It was just habit. If you've weaned ten kids like she has, the old-fashioned way, you automatically think about purées, followed by mash and then small pieces. The idea that the pieces need to be very large was a completely new way of thinking about it for her."
>
> Alex, mother of Amy, 21 months

> "I'd pick Kylie up and her day care provider would say, 'She did eat, but it was more me feeding her, she didn't seem that interested.' I kept saying, 'It doesn't matter if she doesn't eat anything'—but that worry they're not getting enough food is so ingrained."
>
> Marcie, mother of Kylie, 2 years

If, after you've explained how it works, your baby's caretaker is still uncertain about BLW, you may have to reach a compromise to start with. Babies are very adaptable, and, while your baby may find it confusing at first that things aren't the same when she's with someone else, she will quickly learn to expect different things from different people. The most important thing is that her caretaker should respect your views about allowing her to stop eating when she's had enough. If they regularly encourage her to eat more than she needs, she may start to cut down her milk feedings too early and become reliant on puréed foods to satisfy her hunger, which could lead to her becoming frustrated during BLW meals at home.

Mealtime safety

Even if your baby's caretaker is experienced with BLW, it's a good idea to talk through some basic safety points with them so that you both feel confident that your child will be safe. In particular, they need to understand why it is important for babies to be sitting upright and to have someone with them while they are handling food, and why, with BLW, it's your baby who should be in control of what goes into her mouth. If they are looking after other children as well, they need to be alert to the risk of older children putting food into the baby's mouth. They also need to be able to recognize the difference between gagging, coughing, and choking (see pages 62–67) and to respond appropriately. And, of course, anyone caring for babies and small children should have basic training in first aid, in case of emergency.

Sharing Mealtimes

Although you may be at work all day, you'll probably want to make sure that your baby eats at least some of her meals with you. If she is going to be cared for by someone else from before the start of BLW, and you don't want to miss out on any of her early experiments with food, you may be able to arrange for one or two weeks' leave, so you can be the first person to offer her solids. Alternatively, you could try sharing your evening meal with her and letting her have just milk feedings during the day for the first week or so. She won't need to be on regular meals for a few months, and she won't go hungry as long as you don't drop any milk feedings.

Trying to get your baby "onto solids" by a particular date—perhaps to fit in with work, childcare, or vacation plans—isn't a good idea, and it's unlikely to succeed if you're following BLW. If your baby isn't ready, she simply won't take an interest in food, and, if you try to persuade her, she may start to dislike the whole idea. You'll both find the beginning of solid feeding easier and more enjoyable if it happens at the right time for her.

Tips for BLW and childcare

- For the first few days of a new childcare arrangement, it may be a good idea for you to prepare your baby's food in advance. Her caretaker can then see what sorts of shapes are good and which foods are OK to offer. Some childcare professionals assume they should cut food for a baby into bite-size chunks, as they would for a toddler who is using cutlery, rather than into sticks or fingers.
- Discuss with your baby's caretaker how to prepare for the mess and make it safe to give dropped food back to her.
- Share any BLW tips you have discovered and update your baby's caretaker as your baby's abilities and tastes develop—and ask them to do the same for you.

"Looking back, I think a big advantage of BLW was for my parents, who have cared for Natalya while I worked since she was a baby. I know for them it meant that there was no additional food to produce other than extra quantities to feed an extra mouth. I think they were surprised at how simple it was."

Julie, mother of Natalya, 4 years

Breastfeeding when you go back to work

Babies under a year old should still be having plenty of milk feedings. Some mothers express their breast milk so it can be given to their baby while they're at work; others find it easier if their baby has formula when she's with her day care provider or at nursery. Your decision will probably depend on factors such as how many hours a day you will be apart from your baby and how supportive or practical your workplace is. Some babies are happy to go without a milk feeding during the day and catch up with their breast milk intake when they are back with their mother, and many mothers find that breastfeeding morning and evening is a good way to reconnect with their baby when they've been apart all day.

Many parents are surprised by just how adaptable their baby is and how flexible breastfeeding can be. However, if you will be away from your baby for long periods and you don't want to leave expressed breast milk for her, it is better to provide some formula for her caretaker to offer her rather than expect her to suddenly eat more solid food.

For specific advice on breastfeeding and working, talk to your health care provider or a local breastfeeding counselor.

> "I was expressing breast milk at work, so I could see that I was producing less milk, very gradually, as the months went on. By the time Olivia was eleven months, I was only getting a couple of ounces in a day. So I figured I could probably stop the expressing and she could make it up in the evening. She was fine—so we carried on just breastfeeding in the evenings and the mornings."
>
> Farida, mother of Olivia, 2 years

6 A Healthy Diet for Everyone

> "A bonus of BLW for some of the families that I've worked with was that they started to make improvements to their own diets as a result of preparing fresh, nutritious foods for their babies, learning new cooking skills and developing an interest in their family's health."
>
> Julie, public health nutritionist

> "They know when they're having the same food as you and when they're not. And you're very aware that they know this. If you're having ice cream with sprinkles on the top, that's what the baby's having as well. So it makes you think about what you eat."
>
> Mary, mother of Elsie, 23 months

Healthy Eating from the Start

Eating normal family food and being included in mealtimes are at the heart of BLW, so many parents use the introduction of solids to make sure the whole family is eating well. Getting your baby used to having nutritious family food every day will give him the best chance of making healthy eating choices throughout his life.

This chapter is a basic guide to healthy eating for everyone in the family (the foods that are particularly important to limit or avoid in a baby's diet are covered in Chapter 4). Babies learn by copying, so if everyone in the family is eating a good diet, your baby will want to do the same. The kind of food he learns to expect is completely up to you—he isn't yet under any pressure from advertising or friends to eat badly and he's too young to go shopping by himself!

Making an effort to have a healthy diet doesn't mean worrying about your baby's nutrition or trying to control what he eats. For the first few months of solids, very little of his nutrition will come from family food because breast milk or formula will supply most of the nutrients he needs. What matters most is that the food he is offered is healthy and varied, so that when he needs extra nutrients they are readily available to him.

Balancing Your Family's Diet

So how do you make sure your family has a healthy, balanced diet? It's not as difficult as it may seem. Most traditional meals from cultures around the world are fairly well balanced, and a varied diet based on fresh foods with plenty of vegetables and fruit will almost certainly provide your baby and the rest of the family with all the essential nutrients. However, the more you include fast foods, prepackaged meals, and processed snacks in your diet, the more the balance will tip toward too much saturated fat, salt, and sugar and not enough vitamins and minerals.

A diet like this is unsuitable for babies and is linked to the development of heart disease, diabetes, and cancer in adult life.

A balanced diet includes all the nutrients needed for health and is based on the main food groups (see below) in roughly the right proportions. What you eat is likely to vary from day to day, but it can be helpful for adults and older children to aim for a certain number of portions from each group. A portion is roughly the amount that a person can hold in their open hand. However, bear in mind the following:

- Children need proportionately more protein than their parents because their bodies are growing.
- Young children need more fat than older children and adults because their energy needs are higher.
- Toddlers will often eat large amounts of carbohydrates.
- A baby-sized portion is a baby-sized handful. This is much less than many people expect babies to eat. Babies under a year old should still be getting most of their nourishment from breast milk or formula.

What We Need to Eat and Why

The following is a basic guide to the main food groups we need each day, and why.

Vegetables and fruit (five portions daily, preferably three of vegetables and two of fruit), for

- vitamins and minerals, especially vitamin C—for healthy functioning of most of the body's systems, including the immune system,

- fiber—to help prevent constipation and ensure a healthy bowel, and
- simple carbohydrates—for energy and to fight toxins.

Eating a whole fruit provides more fiber and vitamin C, and less damaging sugar, than drinking fruit juice or a smoothie, so choose whole fruits whenever possible (they are cheaper, too).

Grains (including rice, pasta, and bread) and starchy vegetables, such as potatoes (two to three portions daily), for

- complex carbohydrates, providing slow-release energy,
- fiber, and
- vitamins and minerals, especially B vitamins.

Fiber

There are two types of fiber: insoluble and soluble. Insoluble fiber is found in whole wheat products such as whole wheat bread and pasta, wheat bran, and other bran products. Soluble fiber is found in oats, fruit, peas, lentils, chickpeas, and brown rice. Adults and older children need both types of fiber to ensure a healthy bowel. Babies need soluble fiber, but too much insoluble fiber is bad for them (see pages 124–25).

Meat, fish, eggs, nuts, and legumes (one portion daily), for

- protein—for the growth and repair of body tissues,

- iron and zinc—for healthy functioning of all body cells, especially blood and bone (red meat is the best source),
- vitamins A and B—to keep our blood, skin, eyes, and nervous and immune systems functioning well,
- vitamin D and calcium (especially oily fish and eggs)—for bone growth and strength,
- some fat,
- potassium and magnesium—for good metabolism and a healthy heart (nuts are a good source).

Calcium-rich foods (one portion daily, children can have more)
This group includes cow's, sheep's, and goat's milks; fortified plant-based milks; yogurts and cheeses; sesame seeds; green leafy vegetables (except spinach, from which both calcium and iron are poorly absorbed); small, soft-boned fish, such as sardines and mackerel; and dried fruit, such as figs. They provide

- calcium,
- protein,
- vitamins A, B, and D,
- fat (except dried fruit).

Oils and fats (¼ portion daily)
These include animal fats such as butter and fish oil, and oils from plants such as olive, sunflower, and almond, which tend to be more beneficial than animal fats. They provide

- fat, for the healthy functioning of the brain and nerves, and as a concentrated source of energy;
- fat-soluble vitamins A, D, E, and K.

Fats

There are two naturally occurring types of fat: saturated and unsaturated. Saturated fats come mostly from animal sources and tend to be solid at room temperature (for example, butter and lard). The healthiest fats are mono- and polyunsaturated fats, mainly found in plant and fish oils. The two most important polyunsaturated fats are omega-3 and omega-6, which are essential in the diet in small amounts. Omega-6 is found in nut, seed, and vegetable oils; omega-3 is found in fish oils, some nut and seed oils, and breast milk.

Babies need a greater proportion of fat in their diet than adults. If you choose low-fat products for yourself, be aware that some foods that are advertised as low-fat, such as yogurt, contain added sugar, so they may not be the healthy option they appear to be!

Artificially created fats (such as trans fats and partially hydrogenated fats) are often used in ultra-processed foods such as prepackaged meals, factory-baked goods, and snacks. They are thought to interfere with the beneficial actions of healthy fats and increase the risk of heart disease so are best avoided.

Vegetarian and vegan diets

Diets that exclude certain foods risk being low in some nutrients. Meat and fish are key sources of iron and protein, so if you don't eat those foods, you'll need to make sure you're getting the amount you need from other foods. If you don't eat any animal products, you'll also need to be careful to eat foods that contain B vitamins, iron, zinc, and calcium.

Vegetarians can get good amounts of protein from eggs and dairy foods. Soybeans (in the form of tofu, tempeh, soy milk, and textured vegetable protein [TVP]) and quinoa are good sources for vegans and vegetarians. Soy contains high levels of aluminum and plant estrogens so shouldn't be eaten too frequently, especially by babies. Legumes are partial proteins, so they should be combined with grains to provide all the essential amino acids.

Good sources of iron are legumes, such as beans, lentils, and peas; dried fruits such as apricots, figs, and prunes; and most green leafy vegetables (but not spinach). Vitamin C helps with absorption of iron, so including vegetables and fruits that are high in vitamin C with your meals will help to ensure that the maximum amount of the iron available in the food is absorbed.

If you are planning to bring your baby up as a vegan or think you may need to leave out a particular food group, you should discuss what you are planning to offer him with a dietitian or nutritionist. They will be able to advise you how to choose healthy food combinations and tell you if additional vitamin or mineral supplements are needed.

Nutrient sources at a glance

The chart overleaf shows which nutrients are found in which foods. The best sources have the most checks. Some nutrients (for example, vitamin E and selenium) occur in many basic foods, so we haven't listed them individually. Similarly, zinc tends to occur with iron, so it doesn't have a separate entry.

TYPE OF FOOD ⮟	NUTRIENTS ➤	VITAMIN A / BETACAROTENE	B GROUP VITAMINS
Citrus fruits, e.g., orange, grapefruit, mandarin			
Berries, e.g., blueberries and raspberries			
Dried fruits, e.g., apricots, figs, and prunes			
Bananas			✓✓
Other fruits, green peppers			
Red, orange, and yellow peppers		✓	
Avocado		✓	
Green leafy vegetables, e.g., kale		✓	
Root vegetables, e.g., carrots and parsnips		✓ (orange and yellow varieties)	
Starchy vegetables, e.g., potatoes and yams			✓
Legumes, e.g., chickpeas, beans, peas, and lentils			
Soybeans and soy products (including TVP and tofu)			✓✓✓
Cereals/grains, e.g., bread, pasta, wheat, couscous, buckwheat, rice, oats			✓✓✓
Quinoa			✓✓✓
Red meat, e.g., beef and lamb			✓✓✓
Liver		✓✓✓	✓✓✓
Poultry, e.g., chicken, duck, and turkey			✓✓✓
Oily fish, e.g., mackerel, sardines, and salmon		✓✓✓	✓✓
White fish, e.g., tilapia, cod, and sole		✓	✓✓
Eggs		✓✓✓	✓✓✓
Milk and yogurt		✓✓	✓
Butter and cream		✓	✓
Cheese		✓✓	✓✓
Nuts (finely ground), e.g., walnut, almond, and Brazil			
Vegetable, nut, and seed oils, e.g., olive oil, walnut oil, and sesame oil			

VITAMIN C	VITAMIN D/ CALCIUM	IRON	CARBOHYDRATES	PROTEIN	FAT	FIBER
✓✓✓			✓✓			✓✓
✓✓✓			✓✓			✓✓
✓✓		✓✓	✓✓			✓✓✓
✓✓			✓✓✓			✓✓✓
✓✓			✓✓			✓✓
✓✓			✓✓			✓✓
✓✓			✓✓	✓✓	✓	✓✓
✓✓	✓	✓✓				✓✓
✓			✓✓			✓✓
✓			✓✓✓			✓
✓		✓✓	✓✓	✓✓✓ (partial protein)	✓	✓✓
	✓	✓		✓✓✓	✓	✓✓
		✓ (whole grains)	✓✓✓	✓✓✓ (partial protein)		✓✓✓
		✓	✓✓✓	✓✓✓		✓✓✓
		✓✓✓		✓✓✓	✓✓	
	✓✓	✓✓✓		✓✓✓		
		✓✓		✓✓✓	✓✓	
	✓✓✓			✓✓✓	✓✓	
	✓			✓✓✓	✓	
	✓✓✓	✓		✓✓✓	✓	
	✓✓		✓	✓	✓✓	
	✓✓				✓✓✓	
	✓✓✓		✓	✓✓	✓✓	
		✓✓	✓✓		✓✓	✓
					✓✓✓	

Variety Is the Spice of Life!

However well-balanced your diet, it also needs to be varied so it can provide you and your baby with a really broad range of vitamins and minerals. Making sure your baby is offered a variety of foods is one of the most important things you can do to ensure he is well nourished.

Many people buy the same groceries each week; if your shopping list is roughly the same each time, it may be a good idea to start including some new foods. Think about any habits you may have developed with food—many people eat the same thing for breakfast every day or have a rotation of favorite dishes that they eat every week. A diet like this may not be unhealthy, but it won't offer your baby much variety. And if he doesn't like all the foods *you* like, then his diet may become limited as he grows up.

Try the following tips to ensure variety:

- Aim for as many vegetables and fruits as possible of different colors: red, yellow, green, orange, and purple—they each contain different nutrients.
- Try out a few vegetables and fruits you don't normally buy.
- Fresh herbs, such as parsley, cilantro, and basil contain a good range of vitamins and minerals.
- If you use a lot of potatoes, try some other root vegetables such as sweet potatoes or rutabaga.

- Millet, bulgur, couscous, or quinoa can be used in place of rice in many dishes.
- Try rye or pumpernickel bread instead of your usual wheat bread now and again.
- Alternate your usual breakfast cereal with cereals made from a different grain.
- Buckwheat or spelt flour can be used in place of wheat flour in baking and cooking.
- Try nonwheat pasta for a change, such as noodles made from seaweed, zucchini, or rice.
- Chicken, beef, lamb, and pork are all good meat choices, but venison, partridge, rabbit, duck, and goose are also nutritious (though they do tend to be expensive).
- Not all cuts of meat have the same nutrients—chicken legs contain different nutrients from the breast, for example, so vary the cuts of meat you buy.
- Liver is a very good source of nutrients, especially iron. However, it shouldn't normally be eaten more than once or twice a week because it contains high levels of vitamin A, as well as concentrated toxins. Choose organically produced liver when possible.
- While meat is the best source of iron and zinc, we don't need to eat it every day. Legumes such as beans and lentils contain nutrients that animal-based proteins don't. They are also much cheaper.

- Try a vegan cheese, or different varieties of cheese made from cow's, sheep's, goat's, or buffalo's milk.
- Freshly ground nuts and seeds can be added to oatmeal and cereals to increase their nutrient content.
- Flaxseed or walnut oil can be used in a salad dressing or on pasta.
- Avocados contain quite a lot of healthy fat (which is why they're more filling than most other fruits).

Buying Organic

The demand for cheap foods with a long shelf life means that many foods contain chemicals: Crops are often sprayed with pesticides or fungicides and contain artificial flavorings, preservatives, and colors that are commonly added to processed foods. Many of these chemicals are potentially harmful, and there is little research into their combined effects on babies and children.

Foods that are produced organically and don't contain harmful chemicals can be more expensive. Check out your local organic food delivery service; their products are often cheaper than store-bought organic products. A delivery box may even save you money because you won't be tempted to buy unnecessary extras, as you would in the supermarket. Many families prioritize the foods their children eat most often when deciding which organic products to buy.

Unhealthy food—how much is OK?

Many of the foods that are particularly bad for babies are also bad for the rest of the family—adults included. Commercially prepared foods that contain high levels of sugar, salt, or unhealthy fats (for example, cakes, cookies, chips, pastries, pizzas, and pies) aren't really necessary at all and should be eaten in moderation only—maybe a couple of times a week at most. Ultra-processed foods, such as instant meals and sodas, are best avoided completely.

This doesn't mean that your family should *never* have store-bought cakes or cookies, only that they don't provide the best nutrition and risk replacing foods that do. If you don't eat them every day, then your child won't expect to either.

Tips for Getting the Best Out of Your Food

The amounts of nutrients in food aren't set in stone. They can depend on factors such as how the food was produced, how old it is, and how it is cooked. There are plenty of things you can do to make sure you get as much goodness as possible from your family food. The following tips will help you to maximize the available nutrients:

- Buy locally grown vegetables and fruit that are in season, at a farmers market or stand. They will be fresher than imported produce (and may contain fewer preservatives).

Imported foods are likely to have been harvested before they are really ripe, which is also before all the vitamins have fully developed.

- Eat organic vegetables and fruit with the peel on where possible—many of the nutrients are just under the skin. (Nonorganic varieties are best peeled or rinsed with a little diluted vinegar or commercial "veggie wash" to remove superficial waxes and pesticides.)
- Steam vegetables rather than boiling them, to reduce nutrient loss.
- Use any water from cooking vegetables for soups, sauces, and gravy, so the nutrients aren't wasted.
- Cut up vegetables and fruits just before eating or cooking them, as some of the food's vitamin C is lost from cut surfaces, especially at room temperature. Alternatively, cover and refrigerate them. If you are taking food out with you, keep it in a cool bag if you can.
- Frozen vegetables are really useful and contain more vitamins than canned or dried versions. It is also easy to use just the amount you want for each meal, so there's very little waste.

Making sure the meals you share with your baby are as nutritious as possible may start with simply taking a look at what groceries you buy on a weekly basis, and working out what you need to do to make them healthier. Some parents make a whole lot of changes in one go; for example, swapping from supermarket shopping to a farmers market. Others make gradual or smaller changes depending on their circumstances. Some prefer to focus on the way they store and prepare food. Whatever you do, the more nourishing you make your meals, the better it will be for everyone. And if your family is eating healthily, so is your baby.

7 Growing Up with BLW

"When Ellie got to about eighteen months, I realized I was beginning to nag her about food. Not cajoling exactly, but asking her if she'd really finished and didn't she want to try a bit of chicken, etc. And I started to think she wasn't eating enough. I have to keep reminding myself that she still knows what she needs. It's just so ingrained, having to persuade children to eat, and mixing up eating with 'good' and 'bad' behavior."

Sharon, mother of Ellie, 22 months

Maintaining a Baby-Led Approach

As your child grows, it's important to make sure that mealtimes are still enjoyable. Toddlers have a bad reputation when it comes to food, but it's not inevitable for small children to be picky eaters and disruptive at the table—it's just so common that it seems as if it must be normal. There's no need to panic when you hear the horror stories; BLW really can help to prevent many of the problems parents encounter with toddlers and food.

Small children want to assert their will and become more self-reliant and independent, and your child will be happiest where she can succeed on her own and have a sense of achievement. Baby-led weaning is perfect for this—as long as you keep the hands-off approach. Continue to trust your child's appetite, give her only as much help as she genuinely needs, and let her progress at her own pace.

Avoiding Negative Labels

Toddlers are acutely aware of what their parents and others are saying about them and can easily feel they have to live up to any negative descriptions they may hear. Many small children are labeled picky or poor eaters when they are simply making choices about their food or not eating the amounts others expect. True picky eating (where a wide range of foods is rejected) is less likely in children who've been introduced to solid foods with BLW, according to research. Mild food fads and eccentric choices are part of normal toddler behavior.

Your child may choose to eat—or avoid—certain foods for no obvious reason, sometimes for several weeks. As with babies, anecdotal evidence suggests that this can sometimes be related to recent events, including illness, or may even be linked to foods that the child finds difficult to digest or that may trigger an allergic response.

Attempts to persuade or trick your toddler into eating food she doesn't want are unlikely to be successful in the long term, but continuing to offer that particular food occasionally, with no pressure or fuss, will mean that she always has the option to change her mind.

Along with making choices about food that may puzzle their parents, many toddlers eat much less than those around them think they should. But describing them as having a poor appetite is inaccurate and unfair. If a child is well, active, and growing, she is clearly eating enough for her needs—there's nothing poor about that.

Encouraging Self-Service

Older babies and small children usually enjoy serving themselves at the table. Putting everything into serving dishes can be one of the best ways to help you resist the temptation to decide how much food—or which foods—should be on your child's plate. It also encourages conversation and sharing, and, if you have already started fighting with your child over food, it's a good way to help you all enjoy mealtimes again.

Allowing your child to serve herself helps her judge her own appetite; most children are surprisingly accurate when they're allowed to decide in advance roughly how much they are going to eat. So rather than putting your child's portion straight onto her plate, try letting her do it herself. She may need a little help managing serving spoons, but let her choose what to have and how much to take. Remember that she'll copy what you do, so keep an eye on the saltshaker and the hot chile sauce!

As well as helping her judge her appetite, dishing up her own food will give your child valuable lessons in hand-eye coordination, muscle control, measuring, and judging distance and volume. It will also provide her with a sense of control and achievement and will make her feel—and be—more independent. Salads and other cold dishes are ideal to start with. If the food is hot, make sure she can't burn or scald herself, especially if it's something sloppy such as soup or a casserole. And you'll need to ignore the mess she makes the first few times—the more practice she gets, the more skilled she'll become.

> **"Sallyann wants to join in with cooking; she enjoys peeling and cutting and putting things in the pan and stirring them; she even wipes the table. She insists on pouring her own gravy and loves to scrape the pan for second helpings. If we have a casserole, she picks bits out and tells us if she likes them. She'll hold up a bit of zucchini and ask: 'Is this zucchini?' implying that we should know by now that she doesn't like it."**
>
> Anthony, father of Sallyann, 3 years

Small children often like to help themselves to snacks from the cupboard or fridge, too. It can be a good idea to have a small tray of healthy snack foods in containers that your child can open easily, or a fruit bowl that she can reach. If you do encourage your child to help herself to snacks, teach her to sit down and eat her snack with you. Running around while eating can be a choking hazard, and small children should never eat unsupervised.

> "If Hayley is hungry, she just goes into the kitchen and points at the fridge or goes to the fruit bowl and gets an apple or something—she doesn't have to wait until it's lunchtime. And we don't have any unhealthy snacks in the house, so she can have whatever she wants."
>
> Serena, mother of Hayley, 2 years

Toddlers often notice what other children are eating at playgroups or friends' houses and may want the same food. It's best not to make too much of a fuss, even if the food is unhealthy; the odd cookie won't do any harm, and making certain foods forbidden will only make them more desirable (see page 214). If your child is used to healthy food at home, she's more likely to make healthy choices when she's out.

> "Lexie was at a party recently and was helping herself to food. She took a piece of chocolate cake and left most of it. Then she filled her bowl with blueberries, and when she'd eaten them all, she went back for more—she just wasn't bothered by all the cakes and cookies."
>
> Harriet, mother of Lexie, 22 months

Mealtime Behavior

Many parents (and grandparents) worry that a baby who is allowed to play with her food and feed herself with her fingers will never learn proper table manners. But anecdotal evidence suggests that it's babies who are not allowed to experiment with food who are more likely to be disruptive at mealtimes when they are older. Early self-feeding is about exploration and learning. Babies and toddlers need time to acquire the basic skills before they can start to think about fine-tuning their actions to fit in with their parents' ideas of polite behavior. And they need to be included in family mealtimes as much as possible, so that they get to see how others behave.

You are the most important role model for your child, and she is watching you all the time. If you want her to behave in a certain way when you take her to a restaurant, then you'll need to model that behavior at home. For example, try to be consistent about how you eat different foods; if you sometimes eat pizza with a knife and fork and sometimes with your hands, then your child will probably do the same—wherever she is. Children younger than about seven years old can't be expected to understand the subtleties of behaving differently on different occasions or in different settings.

There's no need to praise or scold your child for her mealtime behavior. Young children have a natural desire to copy others and to do what they think is expected of them. If your child senses that her actions have surprised you, she will be confused about what she is expected to do. If you don't like what your toddler is doing, take a moment to think about why she is behaving this way, then try to strike a balance between showing her what sort of behavior is expected at the table and recognizing what her needs are at that particular meal.

Some toddlers become fussy because they dislike sitting in a high chair, possibly because they feel trapped. You may find that your child is happier kneeling on a normal chair or sitting on a booster seat at mealtimes. As long as you can make it safe for her, there's no reason why she can't eat like this.

Young children quickly become bored, especially if they are expected to stay at the table after they have finished eating. They typically start throwing food, banging their cutlery, or trying to get down from the table. This isn't bad behavior; it's simply a sign of boredom and frustration. Toddlers don't like inaction—they want to be busy and they want to be learning. Insisting that a young child stay at the table when she's no longer interested in the food is unrealistic.

Playing at being spoon-fed

Toddlers are naturally playful and enjoy sharing and taking turns. Your child may want to spoon-feed you—or even ask you to spoon-feed her. This is not a sign that she's regressing, or that she has missed out on being spoon-fed, and it doesn't mean she'll want you to feed her all the time. It's just a game.

Tips for encouraging good table manners:

- Whenever possible, eat with your child.
- Be a good role model and be consistent.
- Give her time to learn and don't expect too much too soon.
- Don't make her stay at the table if she has clearly finished eating.
- Don't scold or praise your child—try to see mealtimes from her point of view.

Bribes, Rewards, and Punishments

As your child gets older, it can be tempting to use food as a reward for good behavior, as a bribe to persuade her to do something, or even—by withdrawing certain foods—as a punishment. But linking food with behavior rather than with appetite has the potential to distort her attitude to food and may spell disaster for the management of her behavior in the long term.

Treats for being good may seem harmless enough, but bear in mind that the reward you (or other members of the family) choose to give is unlikely to be a plate of vegetables or a banana—it's much more likely to be chocolates, cookies, or candy. Your child will very quickly begin to see these foods as especially desirable and come to expect them whenever she behaves a certain way. There are three potential problems here: Your child may begin to see chocolate and candy as "better" than other foods, she may start to eat more sugary foods than you would like her to have, and she may start trying to please you only because she wants some cake!

Using food as a bribe or punishment presents similar problems. Once you start saying things such as: "If you eat your carrots, we can go to the playground," or "If you don't finish your sprouts, you won't get any dessert," your child will very quickly become suspicious of vegetables, be convinced they are absolutely second best to dessert, or see eating them as a chore to get through before something better comes along. There's no reason why children shouldn't choose to save a little bit of room for dessert, just as adults do. And, of course, there's no need to offer a dessert course at every meal.

It can be tempting to give children sweet treats to cheer them up when they're crying or upset, but in reality, all these treats do is bribe them to stop crying. A cuddle and a kiss are what they really need. Using food to comfort children risks them confusing the two and may make them more prone, as adults, to seeking out sweet things whenever they feel miserable.

Bribery, rewards, and punishment confuse food with power and control; they're the opposite of what BLW is all about because they interfere with a child's instinct to know what she needs. Using food in this way doesn't work long term anyway: Children quickly see through these ploys and discover ways to regain the control for themselves.

> **"Tom's nearly four and he's got lots of friends whose parents nudge them along when eating, saying, 'You'll get ice cream if you finish your broccoli'—all that kind of stuff. It's so much easier if you just treat it in a matter-of-fact way: It's dinnertime; just eat what you want to eat and don't eat anything you don't want to eat."**
>
> Phil, father of Tom, 4 years

Avoiding an Emotional Battleground

Everybody talks about mealtime battles with toddlers, but they aren't inevitable. Most are the result of a mismatch over what the parent thinks the child needs and what the child thinks she needs. With BLW, this is unlikely to happen, as long as the parents continue to trust their child's appetite and food choices.

Children have a strong survival instinct, especially where food is concerned. They have an extremely reliable sense of when they need to eat, what to eat, and how much. It is up to their parents to trust them. Sometimes parents find it hard to believe that an active eighteen-month-old only needs to eat as much as she did at nine months (or even less)—especially as she was probably having more milk feedings then than she is now. But babies need an extraordinary amount of calories in their first year because their rate of growth is so fast. Although it seems as if toddlers are shooting up, they are not growing at the same rate as they were when they were younger, so they don't necessarily need more food. In fact, if a baby ate as much in her second year as she did in her first, she would be huge!

There is no need to worry about your child's eating now that she's a toddler any more than when she was younger; if she is well and thriving, she knows what she needs. Just make sure the meals you offer are nutritious and well balanced and that she's not filling up on foods or drinks such as cow's milk, juice, or nonnutritious snacks. Most important of all, remember to keep mealtimes relaxed and enjoyable. It's very easy for them to become a battle of wills between parents and child, but battles almost always lead to the child eating even less of the foods the parents want her to eat.

BLW STORY

Baby-led weaning is so easy. Lidia is always happy to sit and feed herself, and she really enjoys mealtimes. Recently a friend asked me to spoon-feed a little girl she was looking after. I couldn't do it—even though I spoon-fed my eldest daughter years ago. It made me feel really uncomfortable after doing BLW with Lidia. The baby was a year old—perfectly capable of feeding herself—and it seemed so wrong. It almost felt like force-feeding.

It feels so much more natural to trust your baby and let them do it themselves. Feeding Lidia this way has changed all my ideas about mealtimes for the coming years. With Jo, my eldest daughter, I was always saying, "Eat up your dinner," and she remembers it. I feel really bad about that now. You just can't do that with BLW. That's a big change of mind-set; I was brought up to believe you can't leave anything on your plate.

I feel much more relaxed at mealtimes with Lidia, and I think that will last throughout her childhood because I've accepted that she decides how hungry she is and what she wants to eat. I'm not going to make mealtimes a battle, and that's really a positive thing.

Lucy, mother of Jo, 16 years; and Lidia, 17 months

Tips for keeping toddler mealtimes baby-led

- Let your child serve herself as much as possible at the table.
- Continue to trust her appetite.
- Let her help herself to snacks (but make sure they're nutritious).
- Avoid using food as a reward, punishment, or bribe, or in place of comfort.

"As soon as Paige turned two, my mom decided it was time we stopped letting her 'have her own way' with food. She'd pretend she was going to eat Paige's dinner if she didn't finish it, and say: 'You're not going to waste all that lovely food, are you?' It was just habit, from feeding her own kids, and it was good-natured—she wasn't trying to bully Paige. But Paige started to be a bit difficult at the table, pushing her food away and so on—but only when Granny was there."

Danielle, mother of Paige, 3 years

Ending Milk Feedings

The natural conclusion to baby-led weaning comes when your child is ready to stop having milk feedings. If she is breastfed, there is no rush for this to happen, and you can let her lead the way. The World Health Organization recommends breastfeeding for up to two years or more, and many children (and their mothers) continue to enjoy the nurturing and health protection that breastfeeding provides until they are well into toddlerhood. Indeed, it is unusual for a baby to give up breastfeeding of her own accord before her first birthday. Your child will let you know when she is ready to stop, either by not asking for the breast or by repeatedly turning away when it is offered. If she can talk, she may simply tell you that she doesn't want to breastfeed anymore.

If you are bottle-feeding, it's more likely that you will take the lead in stopping your child's milk feedings (to help prevent tooth decay associated with bottles). If she's eating family meals, she probably won't need formula much beyond the first year, and toddler formulas are unnecessary. However, she'll still need the cuddles and comfort associated with milk feedings. Many families phase out the feedings gradually, one at a time, and continue to have a quiet cuddle at the times when they would previously have offered a bottle.

However (and whenever) it happens for you and your child, the last feed of breast milk or formula marks the end of weaning. All her nutrition now comes from family food, and the journey that began with her very first mouthful of solid food is complete.

"It all felt so natural with Jack. He's the second child, so I didn't really notice when he started joining in with our meals; it wasn't a big thing. And I never really thought about how long he'd breastfeed for; I just let him decide. It was so easy—there was food and there was boob and he just had what he wanted. By the time he was three, he was hardly having any milk, and one day he kind of looked at me, had a few sucks and that was it. He'd had his last breastfeed—he'd had what he needed; he was done."

Noelle, mother of Rowan, 13 years; and Jack, 10 years

CONCLUSION

We hope you have enjoyed this book and that you have gained insight into why BLW is the logical way to introduce solid foods. You will have seen how it fits perfectly with the natural development of babies' skills, as well as with the other things that they are learning in their first year. Baby-led weaning can help to prevent the sorts of battles over food that are an all-too-common story among parents of toddlers and young children, and it can contribute to making family mealtimes fun for everyone. In a nutshell, it makes eating the pleasure it should be.

Baby-led weaning makes perfect sense as a natural part of growing up. Although children's general development plays a huge part in their ability to feed themselves, what they learn through actively participating in family meals has the potential to contribute to many different areas of their developing personality and skills.

There is a growing amount of evidence that the way children are fed when they are very young establishes the way they will feel about food throughout their childhood, and maybe even into adulthood. Obesity and eating disorders are in the news almost every week, and their consequences can be serious and distressing. Many of these problems have their roots in one (or both) of two key issues: appetite recognition and control. The healthy development of both of these things is at the heart of baby-led weaning.

So much of the advice parents are given about infant feeding is still based on the abilities of three- or four-month-old babies and the assumption that babies need to be spoon-fed. It rarely takes into account the natural abilities of six-month-old babies to take the lead with solids and feed themselves. Baby-led weaning brings together what we now know about when a baby should start solids with what we can see babies are able to do at this age.

We hope we've given you some practical ideas for how to go about using BLW with your own child, how to make it safe and enjoyable, and what to expect as your baby's skills progress. We wish you and your baby many happy mealtimes together.

APPENDIX 1

The Story of Baby-Led Weaning

Although the practice of BLW has probably always existed, the theory of why and how it works was developed by *Baby-Led Weaning* coauthor Gill Rapley.[1] As a public health nurse for over twenty years, she encountered many families who were experiencing problems feeding their babies. At the time, the advice was to start complementary foods by spoon-feeding from four months, but many babies resisted being spoon-fed or would accept only a very limited number of foods. Some parents had resorted to force-feeding to try to get their children to eat, and choking and gagging on lumpy meals were commonly reported. Mealtimes were often extremely stressful for both the parents and their babies.

Gill suspected that the babies were resisting *what was being done to them* rather than the food itself. The simple suggestion to wait a bit longer (if the baby was under six months) or to let the baby try it himself (if he was older) seemed to make a huge difference, both to the babies' behavior and to the parents' stress levels. It all boiled down to giving control back to the baby—which raised the question, "Why did we take it away in the first place?"

As part of her master's degree,[2] Gill recruited a small group of parents with babies of four months (the minimum recommended age for solids at the time) to help her observe what the babies would do if they were offered the chance to touch and handle food without being spoon-fed. The babies were all fully breastfeeding at the start of the study and they continued to be breastfed throughout. The study ended when they reached nine months.

The parents were asked to sit their baby with them at mealtimes and to allow him or her to handle and explore different foods. The babies could eat the food if they wanted to. The parents made short films of the babies' behavior at mealtimes every two weeks and completed a diary of their responses to food and their general development.

The films and diaries showed that, at four months, the babies were not able to pick food up but that they began to reach out for it soon after that. Once they started grabbing it (some earlier than others), they all took it to their mouth. Some gnawed or munched on the food from as early as five months, but they didn't swallow any of it. They all appeared completely absorbed in what they were doing, even though, at this age, they didn't need to eat the food.

By about six and a half months, almost all the babies seemed to have worked out how to get food to their mouth and, after apparently "practicing" chewing for a week or two, they were beginning to swallow it. Gradually they began to play less with the food and their eating became more purposeful. As their hand-eye coordination and fine motor skills developed, they were able to pick up smaller and smaller pieces of food.

By nine months, all the babies were eating a wide range of normal family foods. Most used their fingers to eat, but some were beginning to manage spoons or forks. Their parents reported that they had no difficulties with lumps and they hardly ever gagged while eating. The babies were all willing to try new foods and seemed to enjoy mealtimes.

Gill's later PhD research[3] examined a small group of babies' first encounter with solid food. She compared their responses to being free to handle a piece of cooked broccoli, and eat it if they chose, with being spoon-fed the same food as a purée. What was clear was that these were two very different experiences for the babies. While they were feeding themselves, they were absorbed and interested, but when they were being spoon-fed, they spent most of the time trying to avoid what was happening. It was also clear that their response was to the *way* they were being offered the food, not to the food itself.

At around the same time that Gill was conducting her original study, a great deal of research was emerging to show that, ideally, babies should have nothing but breast milk until they were six months old and that they should move gradually toward a mixed diet after that. Gill's findings, together with the many parents' stories that support them, suggest that normal healthy human babies—like infant mammals everywhere—develop the skills they need to feed themselves with solid foods at just the right age. The findings also suggested that babies are far happier if allowed to follow their instincts and take charge of their own eating.

APPENDIX 2

Basic Rules for Food Safety

Bacteria can spread and multiply quickly in food, and babies are more at risk than adults of becoming ill through food poisoning. Following these simple rules will help keep your family safe:

1. You (and your family)

- Wash your hands with soap and rinse them thoroughly before handling food, especially after touching the garbage can; after handling cleaning materials; after touching pets, their bedding, or food bowls; and after using the bathroom.
- Take extra care with handwashing if you have a cold or a stomach bug.
- Wash your baby's hands with mild soap and water before offering him food and remind older siblings to wash their hands before sitting down to a meal.

2. Surfaces and equipment

- Clean all surfaces and equipment thoroughly before and after you prepare food.
- Clean cutting boards and knives thoroughly after using them, especially after preparing meat or fish. If possible, have a few different cutting boards: separate ones for raw and cooked meat and fish, one for bread, and one for vegetables and fruit. Use a plastic board rather than wood for raw meat and fish.

3. Storage of food

- Follow the storage instructions given on food packages.
- A fridge thermometer can help you check that your fridge is cold enough for most foods. Keep it in the coldest part of the fridge (usually at the back and bottom) and check the temperature regularly. Aim to keep the temperature between 32°F and 41°F (0°C and 5°C). If the temperature is higher, the food will not keep for as long. To keep the fridge at the right temperature, don't leave the door open longer than necessary.
- Don't put hot food into the fridge, as this will raise the temperature of the whole fridge. Overfilling the fridge can raise the temperature, too.
- Put chilled or frozen foods into the fridge or freezer as soon as possible after buying.
- Return any unused chilled and frozen foods to the fridge or freezer as soon as possible.
- Check that stored food is not out of date or not already going bad if it's near its "use by" date.

- Wrap or cover uncooked meat and fish and store them on the bottom shelf of the fridge so that they can't touch or drip onto other foods.
- Food that is not to be eaten right after cooking should be covered, cooled quickly, and put into the fridge or freezer as soon as it is cold. This is especially important for meat, fish, eggs, and rice, all of which can contain germs that multiply rapidly at room temperature. Rice can be rinsed in cold water to cool it quickly.
- There is a theory that the acid in fruit and vegetables can react with the metal in aluminum foil, releasing chemicals into the food, so don't use foil to wrap these foods.
- If you use plastic bags or plastic wrap, check that they are safe to use with food. If in doubt, put the food in a bowl and cover the bowl so that the wrapping doesn't touch the food itself.
- Thaw frozen meat and poultry thoroughly before cooking. It's safer to defrost it slowly in the fridge, or quickly by microwaving, than to leave it sitting at room temperature.

4. Cooking food

- Wash fruit and vegetables before cooking or eating.
- Make sure that food is thoroughly cooked. Before serving, check that it's piping hot all the way through and that meat juices run clear. Don't shorten cooking times given on package labels or in cookbooks.
- Use the recommended oven temperature for oven-cooked foods and follow the instructions carefully if using a microwave.

- Ensure that eggs are kept refrigerated and that unpasteurized eggs are cooked thoroughly, to at least 160° F (74° C). For recipes such as mayonnaise, in which the eggs are raw or undercooked, be sure to use only in-shell, pasteurized eggs.
- If possible, serve food as soon as it is cooked. If you need to keep it hot, make sure that it stays above 145°F (63°C). If you can't keep it that hot, it should be used within two hours or chilled and put into the fridge for reheating later. This is especially important for meat, fish, eggs, and rice.
- Cooked food should be reheated once only. Make sure it is piping hot all the way through before serving.

REFERENCES

Chapter 1: What Is Baby-Led Weaning?

1. *The Compact Oxford English Dictionary*, 3rd ed. (Oxford University Press, 2005).
2. *The American Heritage Dictionary of the English Language*, 4th ed. (Houghton Mifflin, 2000).
3. World Health Organization/UNICEF, *Global Strategy for Infant and Young Child Feeding* (Geneva: WHO, 2002).
4. A. Brown, S. Wyn Jones, and H. Rowan, "Baby-Led Weaning: The Evidence to Date," *Current Nutrition Reports* 6, no. 2 (2017): 148–56.
5. G. Rapley, "Is Spoon-Feeding Justified for Infants of 6 Months? What Does the Evidence Tell Us?" *Journal of Health Visiting* 4, no. 8 (2016): 414–19.
6. G. Rapley, "Are Puréed Foods Justified for Infants of 6 Months? What Does the Evidence Tell Us?" *Journal of Health Visiting* 4, no. 6 (2016): 289–95.
7. A. Brown and M. Lee, "Early Influences on Child Satiety-Responsiveness: The Role of Weaning Style," *Pediatric Obesity* 10, no. 1 (2015): 57–66.

Chapter 2: How Does Baby-Led Weaning Work?

1. World Health Organization, *Guideline: Delayed Umbilical Cord Clamping for Improved Maternal and Infant Health and Nutrition Outcomes* (Geneva: WHO, 2014).
2. L. J. Fangupo et al., "A Baby-Led Approach to Eating Solids and Risk of Choking," *Pediatrics* 138, no. 4 (2016): e20160772.
3. C. M. Davis, "Self-Selection of Diet by Newly Weaned Infants: An Experimental Study," *American Journal of Diseases in Childhood* 36, no. 4 (1928): 651–79.

Appendix 1: The Story of Baby-Led Weaning

1. G. Rapley, "Baby-Led Weaning," in *Maternal and Infant Nutrition and Nurture: Controversies and Challenges*, 2nd ed., ed. V. H. Moran and F. Dykes (London: Quay Books, 2013).
2. G. Rapley, "Can Babies Initiate and Direct the Weaning Process?" (MSc thesis, Canterbury Christ Church University, UK, 2003).
3. G. Rapley, "Starting Solid Foods: Does the Feeding Method Matter?," *Early Child Development and Care* 188, no. 8 (2019), 1109–23.

USEFUL READING

A. Brown, *Why Starting Solids Matters* (London: Pinter and Martin, 2017).

G. Palmer, *Complementary Feeding: Nutrition, Culture and Politics* (London: Pinter and Martin, 2011).

Photo Credits

(All page numbers below refer to the photo insert.)

Page 1
1: Chris Carden
2: Nick Jones
3: Shaun Murkett

Page 2
1: © editoratimo
2: Janice Milnerwood
3: © editoratimo
4: Tracey Murkett

Page 3
2: © editoratimo
3: John Johnston
4: © editoratimo

Page 4
2: Shaun Murkett
3: Amber Rowland

Page 5
1: Cate Garratt
2: Natalie Blechner

Page 6
1: Tracey Murkett
2: © editoratimo
3: Jason Woolfe
4: Fred Coster
5: Fred Coster

Page 7
1: © editoratimo
2: Amber Rowland
3: © editoratimo
4: Natalie Blechner

Page 8
1: Samantha Jones
2: Tracey Murkett
3: Tracey Murkett

ACKNOWLEDGMENTS

We would like to thank everyone who contributed their ideas, experiences, comments, and wisdom to make this book possible. We are particularly grateful to Jessica Figueras, Hazel Jones, Sam Padain, Gabrielle Palmer, Magda Sachs, Mary Smale, Alison Spiro, Sarah Squires, Carol Williams, and Jill Rabin for valuable feedback on the manuscript and for insight, support, and inspiration.

Special thanks go to the many parents who shared their wonderful BLW stories with us; we hope that their experiences of sharing their baby's joy and wonder at discovering food will inspire you as much as they inspired us. We're similarly profoundly grateful to those who sent us photos of their babies' adventures with food—we wish we could have included them all.

Thanks, also, to our editors, Julia Kellaway, Emma Owen, and Becky Alexander for their patience and tolerance, and to Batya Rosenblum for her expert help with the American edition.

Finally, we would like to thank our families for their constant support while we were writing, from reading the manuscript and IT help to photography, babysitting, and making the tea. Our partners, in particular, deserve a medal.

This book is for our children, who continue to teach us so much.

INDEX

A

airway, 63, 64–65
allergies, 120, 126–28
American Academy of Pediatrics, 12, 19
amount of food. *See* quantity of food
appetite control, 37, 59–61, 209–11, 215–19, 222
apples, 103, 123, 131–32, 135, 141–42, 144
artificial flavorings and colors, 119, 144, 202
avocados, 131, 132, 198–99, 202

B

baby corn, 132, 138, 142
baby food (processed), 13, 18, 123
baby-led weaning (BLW). *See also* first foods; nutrition; self-feeding skills
- benefits of, 2, 9, 221–22
- disadvantages of, 41, 100–04
- discovering, 13–15, 16
- expectations, 147–50, 185–87
- healthy food relationships and (*see* food habits and relationships)
- late start for, 113–14
- overview, 2–4, 9–10, 221–22
- popularity of, 19
- readiness for, 11–13, 49, 52, 77–78, 111–12
- for special cases, 70–75
- spoon-feeding vs., 1–2, 8–10, 52, 113–14
- story of, 223–26
- success secrets, 109–10

Baby-Led Weaning Cookbook (Rapley & Murkett), 3
Baby-Led Weaning Cookbook—Volume 2 (Rapley & Murkett), 3
baby's size, 18, 21, 22–23
balanced diet. *See* nutrition
bananas, 103, 132–33, 198–99
battles, at mealtime, 39–40, 163–66, 215–18
beans. *See* legumes
beef, 129, 132, 198–99, 201
berries, 131, 141, 198–99
bibs, 106
biting, into food, 46–47, 84
bowel movements, 172–74
bowls, 107, 177
bran, 119, 125, 141, 194
bread and breadsticks. *See also* grains
- guidelines for, 122, 124–25
- nutritional value of, 194
- serving suggestions, 133–34, 136–38, 141–42, 201

breakfast, 97, 140–41, 149
breast milk feeding
- allergies and, 126, 128
- continuation after solid food introduction, 10, 28, 37, 109
- history of, 16–18
- nutritional value of, 12, 51–56, 109, 111–12, 124, 138–40, 159
- recommendations, 12, 19, 80, 109, 189–90
- self-feeding preparation and, 49, 50, 80, 150–51
- weaning process, 7–8, 166–69, 218–19
- working and, 189–90

bribery, 143, 208–09, 214–15, 218
broccoli, 83, 132
butter, 195–96, 198–99

C

caffeine, 120
calcium, 125, 139, 195, 197, 199
canned foods, 120–21, 126, 204
carbohydrates, 193, 194, 199
caregivers, 97, 185–90

carrots, 131–32, 135, 137–38, 142, 198–99
celery, 138, 142
cereal, 141–42, 201–02
cerebral palsy, 72
cheeses
guidelines for, 119, 121–22, 124
nutritional value of, 195, 198–99
serving suggestions, 202
cherries, 58, 135
chewing
development of, 2, 18, 46–47, 57–58, 66–67
pre-chewing, 130
puréed food as impediment to, 114
readiness for, 24, 49, 225
satiety and, 95
teeth and, 57
chewy foods, 58, 153
chicken, 129, 132, 155, 198–99, 201
childcare, 185–89
choking
cough reflex and, 62, 64–65, 187
gag reflex and, 62–64, 65, 187
hazards, 65–67, 81, 112–13, 143
natural safeguard against, 47
risk of, 61–62
safety precautions, 62, 81, 135, 174, 187, 210
citrus fruits, 126–27, 131, 132, 198–99
clamp-on seats, 104, 182
colds, 157
complementary food introduction. *See* first foods
confidence
baby's development of, 2, 9, 38–39, 88, 96
of parents in baby-led weaning approach, 110–11, 145, 157–61
constipation, 172, 194
conventional solid food introduction. *See* puréed food; spoon-feeding
cooking. *See* meal preparation
coordination development, 2, 38, 47, 67, 72, 84–87
copying, of eating behaviors, 92–94, 97, 109, 114, 152, 212–13
corn, 132, 138, 142
cough reflex, 62, 64–65, 187
crunchy foods, 58, 154–55
cucumbers, 131–32, 138, 142
cups, 107, 139, 174, 175–76, 183
cutlery, 78, 87, 136, 176–79, 183. *See also* spoon-feeding

D

dairy products, 127, 198–99. *See also* cheeses; milk; yogurt
Davis, Clara, 68–69
daycare, 97, 185–90
desserts, 123, 135, 143–44, 214
developmental milestones. *See also* coordination development; self-feeding skills
atypical development and, 46
delays, 72–75
overview, 43–48, 86–87, 224–25
for preterm babies, 70–72
solid food introduction as, 1, 10–11, 14–15, 224–25
dexterity, 2, 38, 47, 67, 72, 84–87
digestive system, 12, 73, 124, 194. *See also* allergies
dining out, 40, 121, 180–84
dips and dippers, 85, 137–38, 142, 153, 177, 179
Down syndrome, 72–75
dried fruits, 141, 195, 197, 198–99
drinks, 107, 120, 123, 138–40, 174–76

E

eating out, 40, 121, 180–84
eating skills. *See* chewing; self-feeding skills
eggs
guidelines for, 126, 229–30
nutritional value of, 194–95, 197, 198–99
serving suggestions, 130, 132, 141
enjoyment, of food, 8–10, 28–29, 39, 109, 110
expectations, management of, 147–50, 185–87

exploration, with food, 37–39, 66–67, 78, 95–96, 109, 110–11
extrusion reflex (tongue thrust), 22, 58

F

fads, 163–66
family mealtime. *See* shared meals
fats
  guidelines for, 119, 164, 192, 196, 203
  nutritional value of, 124, 193, 195–96
  sources of, 139, 141, 142, 144, 199, 202
fiber, 124–25, 141, 194, 199
finger foods, 11, 82–83, 86, 109, 132–34
first foods. *See also* shared meals; *specific foods*
  adaption of, 82–83, 109, 129–38, 189, 204 (*See also* meal preparation)
  allergies and, 120, 126–28
  drinks, 107, 120, 123, 138–40, 174–76
  eating skills (*see* chewing; self-feeding skills)
  enjoyment of, 8–10, 28–29, 39, 109, 110
  experimenting and exploring, 37–39, 66–67, 78, 95–96, 109, 110–11
  false signs of readiness for, 21–22
  flavors of, 35, 150–53
  foods to avoid, 118–24
  guidelines (*see* food safety rules; nutrition)
  history of introducing, 16–20
  instinct for choosing, 54–55, 68–70, 163–66, 215–16
  milk feedings after introduction of, 10, 28, 37, 109
  myths about, 21–25
  nutritional value of, 124–26 (*See also* nutrition)
  overview, 1–4, 117–18
  readiness for, 11–13, 16, 19, 24–25, 52, 59
fish
  fish oil, 195–96
  guidelines for, 119, 125–26, 135, 228–30
  nutritional value of, 194–95, 196, 198–99
  serving suggestions, 132, 135, 155
flavors of food, 150–53
floor protection, 105, 183
food consumed, quantity of, 60–61, 109–10, 115, 156–63, 215–17
food habits and relationships. *See also* food refusal and phobias
  appetite control, 28, 37, 59–61, 222
  development of, 25–26, 113–14, 221–22
  food variety and, 2, 68–69, 87, 200–02
  overview, 191–92
  self-selection by babies, 68–70
food intolerance, 127
food poisoning, 130
food refusal and phobias
  avoiding, 39–40, 156
  developing, 60–61, 91–92, 208–09, 214–18
food safety rules
  for after meals, 92
  choking precautions, 62, 81, 88, 135, 187
  for preparation and storage, 88, 189, 227–30
  for self-feeding, 81–82
food waste, minimizing, 101
forks, 87, 176–79
formula feeding
  with breast milk feeding, 189–90
  continuation after solid food introduction, 10, 28
  history of, 17
  nutritional value of, 12, 53–56, 109, 112, 124
  recommendations, 80, 109, 139

self-feeding preparation and, 49, 158–59
weaning process, 7–8, 166–69, 218–19
frozen vegetables, 204
fruit juice, 120, 140
fruit stains, 103
fruits. *See also specific fruits*
allergies and, 127
guidelines for, 135, 229
nutritional value of, 124, 193–94, 195, 197, 198–99, 202–04
serving suggestions, 83, 130–33, 138, 141–42, 144, 200

G
gag reflex, 28, 62–64, 65, 94, 187
gastroesophageal reflux disease (GERD), 73
grains
allergies and, 127
guidelines for, 119, 124–25
nutritional value of, 124, 194, 198–99
serving suggestions, 136–37, 141–42, 201–02
grandparents, 14–15, 17, 110–11, 185–86, 211
grapes, 131, 135
green beans, 132, 138
green leafy vegetables, 195, 197, 198–99
ground meat, 129

H
hand-eye coordination, 2, 38, 47, 67, 72, 84–87
handwashing, 227
Health Canada, 11–12
health risk factors, 12
healthy food relationships. *See* food habits and relationships; nutrition
heart disease, 12
herbs, 122, 151, 200
high chairs, 78, 81, 103–05, 182
honey, 119
hummus, 85
hunger
assessment of, 111
satisfying by self-feeding, 98, 157–58, 187
satisfying with milk feeding, 21, 50–51, 79–80, 94–95, 114, 167–69
spoon-feeding and, 27, 114

I
illnesses, 37, 120, 157, 164
infections, 12, 119, 130, 157
instinct
food choices based on, 54–55, 68–70, 163–66, 215–16
self-feeding and, 9–11, 44–45, 50–51
International Code of Marketing of Breast-Milk Substitutes (WHO), 13
intolerance, to foods, 127
iron
absorption of, 125
sources of, 54, 55, 129–30, 153, 164, 197, 199, 201

J
juice, 120, 140

K
knives, 176–79

L
lamb, 129, 132
leaning-back position, 66
legumes
as meat substitute, 201
nutritional value of, 124, 194–95, 197, 198–99
serving suggestions, 132, 145, 153
liver, 198–99, 201
lunch, 97

M
mangos, 131, 132, 138
manners, at mealtime, 2, 211–13
meal preparation
adapting first foods, 82–83, 109, 129–38, 189, 204 (*See also specific foods*)
breakfast, 97, 140–41, 149
lunch, 97

for maximizing available nutrients, 204
planning, 3, 39
safety guidelines (*see* food safety rules)
snacks, 142–43, 169–72, 210–11
mealtime. *See* shared meals
meat. *See also specific kinds of meat*
guidelines for, 194–95, 228–30
nutritional value of, 198–99
serving suggestions, 83, 129–30, 132, 135, 201
substitute suggestions, 196–97
mesh feeders, 112–13
messy mealtimes, 41, 78, 100–04, 110
microwave hot spots, 88
milestones. *See* developmental milestones
milk, 139, 195, 198–99. *See also* dairy products
milk feedings. *See* breast milk feeding; formula feeding
modeling of eating behaviors, 92–94, 97, 109, 114, 152, 212–13
motivation, 50–51
Murkett, Tracey, 3

N
nighttime waking, 21
nut butters, 135, 155
nutrition. *See also specific foods; specific nutrients*
guidelines for, 193–99
of milk feedings, 12, 51–56, 109, 111–12, 124, 138–40, 159
organic foods, 202–05
overview, 36–37, 191–93, 197–99
umbilical cord clamping and, 55
variety of foods, importance of, 2, 36, 68–69, 87, 200–02
nuts
allergies and, 126
guidelines for, 81, 135
nutritional value of, 194–95, 196, 198–99
serving suggestions, 141, 202

O
oatmeal, 136–37, 141, 202. *See also* grains
obesity, 59–61, 222
offering food
quantity of food, 89–91, 162, 170
rather than giving, 79–81, 87–88, 115
oils, 195–96, 198–99, 202
oily fish, 125–26, 195, 198–99
older children. *See* toddlers
omega-3 and -6 fatty acids, 125–26, 196
organic foods, 202–05
overfeeding, 89–91

P
parent-led weaning, 8. *See also* spoon-feeding
parsnips, 131, 132, 138, 198–99
pasta, 124–25, 134, 142, 194, 198–99
peanuts, 202
peas, 85, 124, 132, 197
peels, on fruits and vegetables, 204
peppers, 138, 142, 198–99
pickiness. *See* food refusal and phobias
picnics, 98, 184
pincer grip, 45, 47, 85, 87
pit removal, 135
place mats, 107, 182
plate-cleaning behavior, 91
plates, 89–90, 106–07, 183
pooping, 172–74
pork, 129, 132
potatoes, 131–32, 138, 194, 198–99, 200
pouches, of food, 143
poultry, 129, 132, 155, 198–99, 201
pre-chewing, 130
preterm babies, 70–72
processed baby food, 13, 18, 123
processed food, 119, 120–23, 143, 170–71, 196, 203
protein
guidelines for, 193
sources of, 130, 139, 153, 194–95, 197, 199

punishments, 214–15
puréed food. *See also* processed baby food; spoon-feeding
difficulties with, 8–10, 64, 111–12
food relationship development and, 26, 113–14
history of, 18

Q

quantity of food
consumed by baby or toddler, 60–61, 109–10, 115, 156–63, 215–17
offered to baby, 89–91, 162, 170
quinoa, 141, 197–98, 201

R

raisins, 67, 85
Rapley, Gill, 3, 223–26
rashes, 127
raw honey, 119
reactions, to food, 120, 126–28
ready-made meals. *See* processed food
relationship with food. *See* food habits and relationships
rewards, 214–15
rice, 124–25, 134–36, 144, 153, 194, 201
rice cakes, 85, 132, 141, 142
rice milk, 120
runny foods, 58, 107, 136–37, 156. *See also* puréed food

S

safety rules. *See* food safety rules
salmonella poisoning, 130
salt, 119, 120–23, 133–34
satiety response, 2, 28, 161–63
self-confidence. *See* confidence
self-feeding skills. *See also* chewing
confidence and, 2, 9, 38–39, 88, 96
coordination and, 2, 38, 47, 67, 72, 84–87
copying of eating behaviors, 92–94, 97, 109, 114, 152, 212–13
cutlery use, 78, 87, 136, 176–79, 183
development of, 37–39, 44–48, 50, 85
instinct and, 9–11, 44–45, 50–51
motivation and, 50–51
preparation for, 49, 80
safety precautions, 62, 81–82, 88, 135, 187 (*See also* food safety rules)
timeline, 44–48, 86–87
self-selection, of food, 68–70
self-service, of food, 209–11
shared meals
copying during, 92–94, 97, 109, 114, 152, 212–13
enjoyment of, 8–10, 28–29, 39, 109, 110
false signs of readiness for, 21–22
importance of, 14, 19, 74–75
inclusiveness of, 74–75, 78, 80, 109
overview, 108–09
sharing food during, 39, 79, 118, 120, 140
suggestions for, 94–100, 109–10, 188
table manners, 2, 211–13
sippy cups, 175
sitting upright, 62, 81, 103–04
size, of baby, 18, 21, 22–23
slanted cups, 175
snacks, 142–43, 169–72, 210–11
soda, 120
sodium. *See* salt
solid food introduction. *See* baby-led weaning; first foods
soup, 136–37
soybeans and soy products, 120, 197, 198–99
spices, 122, 151, 153
spicy foods, 152, 153
splash mats, 105, 183
spoon-feeding
baby-led weaning *vs.*, 1–2, 8–10, 52, 113–14

choking and, 61, 64, 65–66
defined, 9
difficulties with, 4, 14, 27–34, 59
food phobia development and, 60–61
history of, 18
as playful behavior, 213
as self-feeding interruption, 50
spoons, 87, 176–79
starchy vegetables, 194
storage, of food, 228–29
straining, to poop, 172
strawberries, 126, 127. *See also* berries
sugar, 119, 123, 140, 141–42
swallowing food, 56
sweet potatoes, 131, 132, 138

T

table manners, 2, 211–13
teeth, 57, 120. *See also* tooth decay
teething, 157
textures, of food. *See also* puréed food
chewing development and, 58, 67
exploration of, 37–39
self-feeding skill development and, 85, 87
serving suggestions, 58, 136–37, 153–56
toddlers
baby-led approach with, 207–08, 218
food refusals and phobias of, 36, 156, 208–09, 214–18
mealtime battles with, 215–18
milk feedings for, 218–19
self-serving for, 209–11
tomatoes, 142
tongue-thrust reflex, 22, 58
tooth decay, 120, 123, 140, 171, 219
training cups, 175

U

UK Departments of Health, 11–12
umbilical cord clamping, 55

V

variety of foods, 2, 36, 68–69, 87, 200–02
vegan diets, 196–97
vegetable juice, 140
vegetables. *See also specific vegetables*
guidelines for, 135, 229–30
nutritional value of, 193–94, 203–04
serving suggestions, 83, 130–33, 138, 142, 200
vegetarian diets, 196–97
vitamin A, 139, 195, 198, 201
vitamin B, 139, 194, 195, 197, 198
vitamin C, 193–94, 197, 199, 204
vitamin D, 125, 139, 195, 199
vitamin E, 195, 197
vitamin K, 195
vitamin supplements, 125
vomiting, 94

W

waking, at night, 21
wasted food, minimizing, 101
water, 138–40
weaning, 7–8, 10. *See also* baby-led weaning
weight gain, 18, 21, 22, 110
wet-nursing, 16–17
wheat, 127
white fish. *See* fish
window of opportunity, for solid food introduction, 59
World Health Organization (WHO), 11–12, 13, 19, 218–19

Y

yogurt
guidelines for, 123, 124, 196
nutritional value of, 195, 198–99
serving suggestions, 136–37, 141, 142, 144

Z

zinc, 54, 118, 195, 201

ABOUT THE AUTHORS

GILL RAPLEY is known worldwide as the pioneer of baby-led weaning, having developed the theory while studying babies' developmental readiness for solids as part of her master's degree. She subsequently gained a PhD for her research comparing spoon-feeding with self-feeding. Gill has been a public health nurse, midwife, IBCLC, and voluntary breastfeeding counselor. As well as writing with Tracey Murkett, she is the coauthor, with Jill Rabin, MS, CCC-SLP/L, of *Your Baby Can Self-Feed, Too*. Gill lives in Kent, England, with her husband. They have three grown children and one grandchild.

TRACEY MURKETT is a writer, journalist, and breastfeeding peer supporter. After following baby-led weaning with her own daughter, she wanted to let other parents know how enjoyable and stress-free mealtimes with babies and young children can be. She lives in London with her partner and their daughter.

Gill and Tracey are also the authors of *The Baby-Led Weaning Cookbook: Delicious Recipes That Will Help Your Baby Learn to Eat Solid Foods—and That the Whole Family Will Enjoy*; *The Baby-Led Weaning Cookbook—Volume 2: 99 More No-Stress Recipes for The Whole Family*; and *Baby-Led Breastfeeding: Follow Your Baby's Instincts for Relaxed and Easy Nursing*.

ALSO AVAILABLE

Your Baby Can Self-Feed, Too
Adapted Baby-Led Weaning for Children with Developmental Delays or Other Feeding Challenges

By Jill Rabin, MS, CCC-SLP/L, and Gill Rapley, PhD

$17.95 US | $23.50 CAN | 288 pages | 16-page color photo insert
Trade paperback: 978-1-61519-902-0 | Ebook: 978-1-61519-903-7

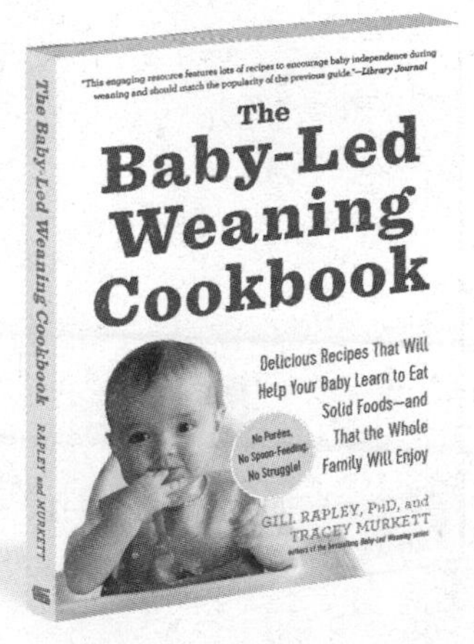

The Baby-Led Weaning Cookbook
Delicious Recipes That Will Help Your Baby Learn to Eat Solid Foods—and That the Whole Family Will Enjoy

$16.95 US | $21.95 CAN | 192 pages | 73 color illustrations
Trade paperback: 978-1-61519-049-2 | Ebook: 978-1-61519-168-0

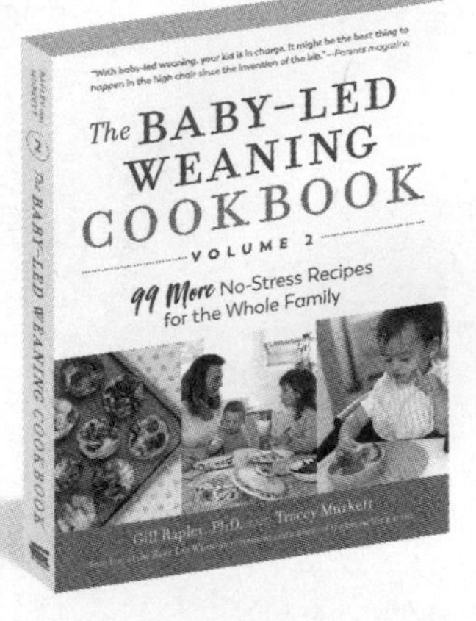

The Baby-Led Weaning
Cookbook—Volume 2
99 More No-Stress Recipes for the Whole Family

$16.95 US | $21.95 CAN | 192 pages | 46 color photographs
Trade paperback: 978-1-61519-621-0 | Ebook: 978-1-61519-623-4

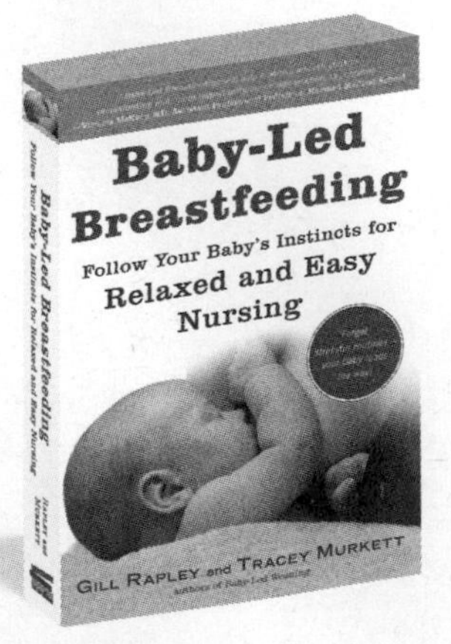

Baby-Led Breastfeeding
Follow Your Baby's Instincts for
Relaxed and Easy Nursing

$14.95 US | $22.95 CAN | 320 pages | 8-page color photo insert
Trade paperback: 978-1-61519-066-9 | Ebook: 978-1-61519-164-2